D1542564

ADVANCE PRAI

LESSONS FROM KATHERINE

Lessons from Katherine is a must-read for professionals who take care of children with disabilities, so that they might appreciate how their words and actions can both build up and tear down parents who are facing these challenges. Likewise it is a book that will help all who want to know how to reach out to family or friends who are parenting a child with disabilities and those parents who are riding the rollercoaster themselves.

Dr. Margaret McBride MD
Clinical Neurophysiologist, Akron Children's Hospital - Akron, OH

One of the gifts of this very personal and vulnerable book from clergywoman and parent, Glenda Prins, is that the "lessons" learned come both from the pain and struggle of raising a young girl with multiple disabilities and from the transforming moments where an unexpected phrase, insight, symbol or experience lead to revelations of strengths, love, and the presence of God. Many readers, especially parents, will say 'I have been there' and others, like clergy and professionals, will be able to use the book to say, 'Let me be there more care-fully in the future.'

The Rev. William Gaventa M.Div.
Director of Community and Congregational Supports at the Elizabeth M. Boggs Center on Developmental Disabilities, and Associate Professor, UMDNJ-Robert Wood Johnson Medical School, New Brunswick NJ

This is an extraordinary book. At times joyous about the author's beautiful child, Katherine, and at times achingly sad about the child's disability which changes all their lives. There are no easy platitudes here about blessing God for giving them this chance to nurture their child. Their struggles will stay with the reader long after the last page.

Margrett McFadden
Retired Chairperson of Penfield School Libraries, Penfield, New York

Written with soul-depth feelings and refreshing honesty, *Lessons from Katherine* conveys to the reader the challenges, pain, and unique joys inherent in parenting a child who contends with major disability. Insights into working together within a marriage, the role of professionals, the support of people who care for us, and the struggles of reconciling our faith with reality, even within the heart of a pastor are provided. But more than anything, this book carries us into the realm of unconditional love.

Lawrence Nazarian MD
Pediatrician *(retired)* Rochester, NY

This is a story about one family's incredible life journey. How they came to terms with their adopted child's disability; and the affect it had on their lives as husband and wife. Their hope and determination to make their situation work, as well as their resilience in the face of so many obstacles made it possible for them to effectively achieve their goals.

Susan Gornall
Member, Mountain Rise United Church of Christ, Fairport, NY

Lessons from Katherine is both compelling and illuminating. Its stories and reflections make for gripping reading, while laying bare the needs of families raising children with disabilities and the strategies that help them navigate this most difficult challenge. Parents will see in these pages a reflection of their own dreams and struggles. Pastors and counselors will gain insight into what helps and what hinders the full participation of disabled persons and those who care for them. A must-read for anyone who seeks to build whole, healthy, inclusive families and communities!

The Rev. Martha Koenig Stone
Associate Pastor, Henrietta United Church of Christ, Henrietta, NY

As I read *Lessons from Katherine*, I laughed, I cried, and I was inspired. As a professional who works with individuals with disabilities, I had a personal connection with Katherine and her family. Glenda Prins did not keep anything back when writing this. I recommend reading *Lessons from Katherine*." If you have a family member with a disability, or you support a person with disabilities, this book will put a new light and deep understanding on your work.

Lindsey Wollschleger
Manager, Jennifer Lane Group Home, Heritage Christian Services, Inc., Rochester, NY

I thoroughly enjoyed reading *Lessons from Katherine*, and could hardly put it down as the story unfolded and the emotions drew me in. The feelings portrayed were genuine and from the heart, a story of God's grace in the midst of disappointment and struggle. The love that Katherine's family came to experience because of this special child's life is a testimony to us all.

Gail Elenbaas
Director, Coffee Break Ministries Dearborn, Michigan

This courageous, clearly written book challenges us to think how we love, how we survive, how we keep the faith. The author tells us how one family member or circumstance affects everyone—for generations. Thank you for daring to share.

Martha Tollers
LMSW, Family Therapist *(retired)*, Rochester, NY

DEDICATION

In Memoriam

Katherine Wierenga Prins
December 23, 1977 – September 14, 2010

it was all for Love's sake

Lessons from Katherine

Spiritual Struggles Series

Lessons
from Katherine

Spiritual Struggles Series

Glenda W. Prins

To Kathy—
many blessings!
Glenda Prins

Circle Books

Winchester, UK
Washington, USA

First published by Circle Books, 2013
Circle Books is an imprint of John Hunt Publishing Ltd., Laurel House, Station Approach,
Alresford, Hants, SO24 9JH, UK
office1@jhpbooks.net
www.johnhuntpublishing.com
www.circle-books.com

For distributor details and how to order please visit the 'Ordering' section on our website.

Text copyright: Glenda W. Prins 2012

ISBN: 978 1 78099 451 2

All rights reserved. Except for brief quotations in critical articles or reviews, no part of this
book may be reproduced in any manner without prior written permission from the publishers.

The rights of Glenda W. Prins as author have been asserted in accordance with the Copyright,
Designs and Patents Act 1988.

A CIP catalogue record for this book is available from the British Library.

Design: Stuart Davies

Printed and bound in the USA by Edwards Brothers Malloy

We operate a distinctive and ethical publishing philosophy in all
areas of our business, from our global network of authors to
production and worldwide distribution.

CONTENTS

1. Early Days — 1
2. Struggling to Breathe — 17
3. God Only Knows — 26
4. A Little Shaking in her Arms — 33
5. The Long Haul — 44
6. Turning the Corner — 54
7. The Same and Different — 62
8. Fire in her Eyes — 75
9. Life Expectancy — 85
10. Chilled — 90
11. Second Year — 106
12. Listening for Grace — 116
13. Wise Child — 126
14. Little Pockets of Mystery — 136
15. You Are You — 145

Epilogue — 152
Acknowledgements — 156

Authors note: Some names have been changed.

Yes, within that broken child, a light is shining.
Jean Vanier

Chapter One

Early Days

I entered our apartment, ebullient. It was a delicious spring day in Ann Arbor: the air streaked with sunlight, buds making their appearance, Frisbees flying, and spirits soaring. But I was happy for a different reason: I'd just returned from a visit to the University of Michigan Health Service where I'd taken a pregnancy test. This was before the days of the immediate response home tests. In 1972, we still had to wait at least 24 hours for the rabbit to do whatever he was going to do.

The whole pregnancy thing was mostly carelessness on our part, nothing we had planned, but it didn't matter. Tom, my husband, and I began singing jingles to each other about the baby on its way, as we danced around our apartment.

At the Health Service, I had been reserved, certain that the healthcare practitioners would see how foolhardy this possibility would be. Tom was in graduate school; I was working for a pittance at a dead-end job. But despite the difficulty a pregnancy would present to us, we were happy. Becoming parents might be a challenge at ages 22 and 23, with no immediate, solid job prospects, and an unfinished graduate degree, but both of us knew we wanted children. It was just part of the deal. We hadn't planned for our family; the expectation that we would have a family was simply a part of the background noise of our marriage. So we floated around our little apartment that night, feeling silly, giddy with delight that we were going to have a baby!

Until I returned to the Health Service. I had been surprised that they insisted I return in person for the results—why couldn't I hear the news in a convenient little phone call?—but that was the rule and so I went back. The test was negative. I was hugely disappointed, and yet couldn't really show it. The nurse said quietly, 'I'm glad it's the answer you wanted.' It wasn't, but I didn't know how to name it. As much as I wanted a baby, I felt guilty for wanting one, guilty for not planning and feeling utterly inept in my life. Three days later, I got my period.

Tom and I met the first semester that I attended Calvin College, a small liberal arts college in Grand Rapids, Michigan. We were 'Thespians' and sat next to each other on the way home from a bus trip to the Stratford Shakespeare Festival in Ontario, Canada. In the back of the bus, a small group of seniors were singing loudly, '*There were bells on the hill, and I never heard them ringing . . . till there was yooouu.*' When we stopped along the way, Tom bought my hot chocolate. And that was it. We were an item.

We broke it off, briefly, mostly because I didn't want to meet my parents' expectations (Go to Calvin College, meet a Christian boy of Dutch descent, marry) so quickly. He was a sophomore to my freshman. He was a Grand Rapids boy; I was a dorm student from Chicago. We married between my junior and senior year and headed to Chicago, where Tom was already enrolled in a graduate program in Russian history. After six months in Chicago, we moved back to Grand Rapids so I could finish my degree. Nine months later, we landed in Ann Arbor, where he enrolled in a graduate program in medieval history at the University of Michigan.

If it sounds peripatetic, it was. We bounced around in those years, neither of us terribly focused. I felt like I cut a bargain with Tom: I'll work at whatever job I can get while you finish your degree. Then you can support me! I imagined a life in which I cared for small children and did art projects while Tom worked as a distinguished professor of history at an idyllic college. I had very little sense about a career or vocation for myself. Marrying Tom had been a way for me to avoid the issue.

I look back at that time and often feel that 'Gunnah teach?' was the sum total of the vocational guidance for women at my college in the late sixties and early seventies. It didn't serve me well. I slid registration each term by signing up 'Pre-seminary' and 'Greek major' until my senior year. I thought I was being absurdly funny, since no woman that I knew ever darkened the door of Calvin Seminary. Neither was I ever asked by a member of the faculty or administration about my program choices, and I think I was the only one that got the joke. What a ridiculous thing to think! A woman signing up as 'pre-sem' was so out of the range of the possible as to become invisible. I ended up with a degree in art and philosophy, and the day that my signed diploma appeared in my mail box, I'd spent eight hours stuffing envelopes.

But the bargain didn't work out very well. Tom wasn't finishing; he racked up as many incompletes as finished courses. (He did eventually earn an M.A. in history.) Meanwhile, I toiled away at a variety of low-level clerical jobs for the university, and took ceramics classes at Eastern Michigan University in Ypsilanti. Later, I became the secretary of the small chapel where we worshipped. Eventually Tom left school and his part-time job at a local bookstore and opened his own Ann Arbor shop, Paideia Books.

The best parts of those early years were the friendships we made and developed. We took time on the weekends to go to the movies or out for supper; we had friends over and visited them. Several of our friends had small children. Whenever children were around, Tom and I gravitated to them. Joey, Peter, Anna, and Andrew were our little friends, and we delighted in seeing them.

After a few more years of intermittent health care, a friend suggested I seek out her gynecologist. By this time, we were thinking more consciously of beginning a family, although still with some ambivalence because our income remained abysmally low. I prepared for my appointment by attempting to keep track of my basal temperature. Dr. Morgan was fairly stern. She didn't like the notes I'd kept and quickly assigned one of her assistants the job of collating my numbers into a chart. Then she turned to me and warned me that I had better be careful unless I was absolutely sure I was ready to have a baby. 'If you're careless,' she scolded, 'you might just get pregnant.'

But I knew that we were already being 'careless' and that we weren't getting pregnant, and I was already deeply afraid that getting pregnant was not going to be easy—or even possible for Tom and me. My ambivalence was beginning to be more about the fear that we wouldn't be able to conceive as that we would. We were genuinely careless in the 'protection department,' coming together without the consistent aid of birth control. The doctor scheduled a few medical tests for me and ordered a sperm count for Tom. We took the tests, held our breath, and waited.

When I called the medical office to get the results, the nurse quickly put me on hold while she raced to get the doctor. Dr. Morgan came on the line and informed me that Tom's sperm count was zero. She had already made arrangements for us to see a urologist and gave me his number. And then, having placed the responsibility for informing Tom squarely on my shoulders, she gave me advice that haunts me to this day.

'Be very gentle with him,' she counseled softly. 'This will be very hard for him to hear, so you'll need to be very, very careful as you tell him about this.'

'What about me?' I wanted to scream. 'What about me?' But I didn't scream. Instead, I listened in stunned and agonized silence. My hopes were being dashed just as surely as Tom's, and now it had become my job to help him without any mention of the shock and grief that I was experiencing. Didn't she think to invite us back to her office for the results, to tell us together and face to face that we would have a great big sorrow?

Several years later, as a dear friend dealt with infertility, her doctor told her in definite tones, 'The next time you come, I want your husband to come with you,' clearly pulling the two of them together as they dealt with difficult news. That didn't happen for us, and I believe now that giving me the task of telling Tom myself, as well as withholding support for me, caused us lasting pain that made the process of working through our grief even more difficult than it needed to be.

When Tom came in that evening, he knew from looking at me that something was very, very wrong. We were living in a little second-floor apartment at the time, three rooms carved out of what was once a single family home. I had painted the cabinet doors orange and purple and yellow to match the wild curtains I'd hung at the windows. I heard Tom's step on the stairs and went to meet him.

I'm not good at holding things in with him; I blurted out the test results. I know I stumbled over the words; tears leaked out of our eyes. We were mostly silent as we sat at our little kitchen table and swallowed our dinner. We made plans to contact the urologist to set up Tom's appointment. We were numb. Numb with the shock of this loss, numb with our loneliness, and agonized by this fresh new wound. In a way, we were holding ourselves together so that we could gather the information we would need to move forward. But in that moment, the clock stopped. We could only wait and try to hope.

Meanwhile, our friends were having babies. All around us, friends, family members, and acquaintances were vigorously procreating, becoming 'fruitful and multiplying' with an ease I could barely imagine. They held up beautiful children with that gleaming look that says, 'Look! Look! Look what we produced.' Though I had earlier relished my time with the children of friends, now I became increasingly more jealous. We could only stand and watch.

Our friend Nick asked Tom if our parents were pushing for grandchildren.

'They did for a while,' Tom said, 'but they stopped.'

'Why did they stop?' Nick asked.

'Because we told them we couldn't have children.'

There it was—the cold painful truth. Tom and I couldn't make babies. We felt shamed by our obvious failure to complete an assignment that seemed so easy to everyone else! What was wrong with us that no baby was growing in my belly?

I knew by this time that I wanted nothing more than to become a mother. Actually, what I wanted was to get pregnant. I wanted to be able to strut around with a great big belly that no one would call fat, wearing adorable maternity outfits with tucked bodices and full skirts, absorbing the reverence due gestating women. I wanted to make my own baby.

Tom and I kept the urologist appointment together. As we approached the intake desk, the doctor's secretary greeted us when we were twelve feet away. In a loud voice, she asked, 'Are you here for the vas?'

Tom and I looked at each other and gulped. I think I may have spoken first. 'What? What did you say?'

'For the vas. Are you here for the vasectomy?'

'Uh, uh—for the other thing,' I squeaked out.

Tom was handed a clipboard asking for essential information, and set to filling it out. It was only a short time before we were ushered into the doctor's office. He wanted Tom to give him a semen sample first, and then we would meet with him a few minutes later.

Tom complied and came back to sit next to me in the waiting area. The doctor's office door was open and we could hear him discussing his portfolio with his stockbroker. The doctor's secretary was not the only one with a loud voice! I don't know how long we waited; it seemed interminable because we just wanted to beat it out of there.

Finally we met, and the doctor suggested a testicular biopsy, holding out the possibility of microsurgery. Tom did have the biopsy, but he was told he would not be a good candidate for the surgery. When these processes proved fruitless, we were back at square one: no baby, no pregnancy, no hope.

My primary care physician told me that we might get help through artificial insemination by donor and sent us to a clinic in suburban Detroit. My heart swelled with the hope that this might work for us. Tom wasn't crazy about the idea, but he's a good sport, and he joined me on our first visit. Meeting with the doctor, we learned that the medical procedure is fairly straightforward; using donated sperm, I would be inseminated and have a natural pregnancy. The doctor suggested that this was better than adoption because it could control for the drug usage that was increasingly harming infants available for adoption. The sperm donors would be screened for intelligence, looks, and a positive family medical history. Also, the baby would carry my genetic makeup. Then he described the tests which would determine how good a candidate I was and the processes to get started.

We were more interested in the emotional and spiritual aspects of donor insemination. What do you tell the child about his/her origins? How do you talk about this within your family? The doctor was less than helpful. 'We tell families never to talk about this,' he said. 'It's no business but your own.' Then he went on to say that younger couples treated donor insemination as they might a blood transfusion, and that he knew it was effective because numbers of couples were returning to the clinic for their second, third, and fourth children. 'Just think of it as receiving a protein,' he counseled.

When we left the clinic, I was still buoyed by the idea of pregnancy and childbirth, but Tom was very discouraged. Even with my relentless drive for pregnancy, I felt puzzled. I knew myself as a person who liked to 'understand' things, who would rather talk about emotional experiences than bury them. I wasn't sure AI would work for us. But information is power. I decided to return for the initial set of tests which would determine whether or not I was even a good candidate for the procedure. If

I was, we'd continue the conversation. If I wasn't, case closed and the decision would be made.

For this visit, I drove alone to the clinic. That day, I had to wait well over an hour to see the doctor. The waiting room was quiet; during most of my wait, I was alone in the room. That gave me plenty of time to peruse the photo albums that filled the office waiting room. Each album was brimming with adorable baby pictures, each baby cuter than the last. It seemed to me that many of the babies shared facial features that were similar to the doctor we had first interviewed. I'd look at one, then the next, wondering if I was imagining things or whether that doctor really was the number one sperm donor in the clinic. At a hundred dollars a pop, it would have been a nice way to boost his income.

Finally, I was led into a small examining room and set up on the table with the stirrups and the humiliating paper gown. Another long wait ensued. This time a different doctor breezed into the room. He began the exam, talking not to me, but to the nurse whom he was regaling with stories of his latest squash game. When he did finally speak to me, he assumed that we were going full steam ahead with this project.

I interrupted him. 'We haven't completely decided that we're going to go through with this.'

'Then what are you doing here?' he roared.

'Well, if I'm not a good candidate and we know that, then the decision is over. But if I am, then we'll have something to talk about. Either way, we'll have the information.'

At this he growled. He finished the exam as quickly as he could and strode out of the room. His nurse meekly followed. I felt deeply upset by the way I had been treated as I put myself back together and headed to check out. No one was at the check-out desk, but there were numerous signs that demanded payment when services were rendered. I got out my checkbook and waited. And waited. Finally, I walked out the door.

And then they noticed me. A clerk or nurse ran after me and

brought me back to the desk. I was visibly shaking as I wrote out a check. The doctor who had examined me appeared in the window. 'Mrs. Prins, is something wrong?' he asked.

'Yes,' I sputtered. 'You kept me waiting. You didn't want to answer my questions. You were angry that we hadn't made up our minds.'

'Let's go into the examining room to talk.'

He led me back to the room where I'd just been examined.

'I waited over an hour and a half and then you raced through the appointment. You got mad at me because we're still making our decision. You didn't want to answer my questions.'

'I'm tired. I was up all night delivering a baby.'

'Well, if you're too tired to keep appointments, reschedule them. This wasn't an emergency situation.'

By this time, my voice was increasing in pitch and volume and he appeared uncomfortable.

'Keep your voice down,' he hissed.

Telling me to shut up has the opposite effect on me. I raged. I ranted. I fumed. I shouted.

'Well, I was all alone out there; I felt like an animal when you examined me . . .'

He cut me off. 'Well, it's what we do to animals. We inseminate cows!'

The interview was over. I raced out of the office and drove home as fast as I could, tears streaming down my face the whole way. Artificial insemination was not going to work for us. Tom's reluctance combined with my bad experience created a barrier that we could not overcome.

All that was left was adoption. I have cousins who were adopted, cherished members of my own family. Tom's mother and father had been foster parents for an adoption agency, and his younger sister was adopted. We were interested and we were not unwilling, but we were afraid of the process, because by this time our self-esteem was so low as to render us terrified that if we engaged in a family study, we would surely be declared unfit.

Our friends, Wayne and Nelva, adopted a beautiful child, Martin, from Columbia. After only a six-month process, they went to South America to bring home their baby. Martin was a charming child, sweet and cuddly and interested in the world. As we spent time with them, they began to encourage us to consider an adoption through Columbian American Friends.

One weeknight, when Nelva knew Tom would be out of town, she and Wayne invited me for dinner. As soon as dinner was over, she cut to the chase. 'Come with us,' she said. 'We're going to a meeting of CAF.' Reluctantly, I allowed myself to be dragged along to the gathering. Midway through the meeting, as we sat surrounded by beautiful Columbian children, Nelva turned to me with a devilish grin.

'Oh, Glenda,' she sighed. 'Aren't they amazing? Aren't they just beautiful?'

'Oh Nelva,' I responded, 'you are sooooo subtle.'

Fearing that adopting from CAF might move too swiftly, Tom and I finally began the slow process of a domestic adoption. We chose an agency that was connected with our church, the same agency for which Tom's mother had fostered many babies. The process was that you could call every six months. Eventually, your names would move up the list and you would receive *an application*! After about a year and a half, we got ours. Even though we'd called regularly over a year and a half, when we actually got the application, we waited so long to fill it out, the agency finally called *us* to see if we were still interested.

That lit a fire under us; we filled out the application, lined up our recommendations, and then composed a lovely letter about how important this was to us, how we were taking the process seriously and thoughtfully. We made several trips to Grand Rapids, Michigan, where we met with a social worker. As people who had never had to relate to social workers, this was a new experience. We felt vulnerable being put under a social microscope: they looked into our marriage, our psyches, our finances. Then to our utter and total amazement, they approved us for adoption.

The news was good, but it was still uncertain. There was no telling when this adoption might actually occur. We'd heard enough horror stories about the adoption carpet being pulled out from underneath people's feet at the last minute that we were afraid to get too excited. I bought two stuffed toys and made a small quilt, but other than that, we weren't taking much action. I was still working at the Campus Chapel at the time, and continued to pour my energies into my very part-time job and full-time volunteer work. Tom had opened a small, scholarly bookshop, Paideia Books, and that work consumed him quite thoroughly.

Late in March, on Good Friday, we got a phone call. There was a little girl waiting for us. We were overwhelmed with joy! I remember that afternoon, heading over to a performance of the Bread and Puppet theatre with some of my colleagues. I was completely elated. On Sunday, Easter Sunday, we stood up in our small congregation and told them the good news! We'd had a resurrection of our own that Easter, thrilled by the prospect of welcoming a baby girl into our home.

The few days before we met her were a total blur. We called friends and family with our good news. The deal was we got to see her on a Wednesday afternoon; then we would come back the next week to bring her home. We were frustrated that they were going to make us give her back after we met her, but it turned out to be helpful — we still had to purchase furniture and clean out the room that would become her nursery.

On the first drive down to Grand Rapids, we spent the entire trip debating the relative merits of Katherine with a 'K' or Catherine with a 'C.' We chuckled to ourselves as we made up stories with her name in them: 'Oh, Katherine went with Tom to the store.' 'Katherine had a good day at school today.' She was becoming a person to us, a person we would know and love. In the end, 'K' won out, and we were ready to provide information for the new birth certificate that would be generated for her, listing us as her parents.

Parents! That was the thing. We were going to be parents. The dream would not be fulfilled in the way we had first imagined, but it was coming true. When we arrived at the agency, we were led into a small room that held a couch, a chair, and a small bassinet. And in the bassinet was the most beautiful baby we'd ever laid eyes on. She looked up at us with her own big blue eyes and just the hint of a smile. She was alert and curious, and amazingly comfortable in our arms. We had about an hour to hold her, feed her from the bottle the agency had prepared for her, and basically just grin at each other from ear to ear. We could hardly believe it! This beautiful child would be ours.

After an hour or so, the social worker came into the room, followed by another agency staffer, who whisked Katherine away so quickly we could barely focus. We made plans to return in a week and headed home.

Now we whirled into action. We still had furniture to purchase and a desk to clear out of the soon-to-be nursery. We went downtown and shopped at the children's store on Main Street. Never had we giggled so much on any shopping trip. We came home with bibs and crib sheets and little PJs. I made a little dress just for the day we would bring her home.

My cousin invited us for dessert on Monday night. I thought nothing of this, but Gwynn had organized a surprise baby shower for me in the space of a few days! Her living room was filled with good friends, lots of love, and a pile of presents.

At last the day arrived. We got up early and dressed carefully. And then, off we went—to bring home our daughter and start the next chapter of our lives. We drove to Grand Rapids, where we were met by both sets of parents—Tom's from Grand Rapids and mine from Chicago. Our families were ushered into a small conference room, while Tom and I went to meet in our social worker's office.

In his office, we set to work signing the legal documents that would certify her adoption. An agency worker we did not recognize plopped ten pounds of gorgeous baby girl into my arms, with Tom at my side. *Who is this baby?* I wondered. *Where are her parents?* I was startled to realize that now *we* were her parents. This little baby and I were strangers to each other, but that moment sealed me to her forever as mother and daughter.

Finally, we could join our families in the little conference room. The social worker led the group in prayer, and then read the Old Testament text about Hannah praying for a child and becoming Samuel's mother. I remember thinking, 'This is an odd choice. Hannah actually gets pregnant,' but I kept my lips zipped and suffered through the little ceremony as the price of adoption. We posed for pictures with our family and our new baby and went to Tom's parents' home, where his mother had prepared a lunch for us.

At lunch we were joined by dear friends, Joel, Rosanne, and Grace. We passed Katherine around and around. She was utterly irenic. Just as sweet as you please and gentle; she didn't cry or fuss, just contentedly let everyone have their turn. Joel and Rosanne had adopted their daughter, Sharon, two years earlier. Rosanne commented that Katherine was such an easy baby. 'By this time, Sharon was falling apart and howling!'

We all agreed Katherine was a perfect baby. We opened gifts, we laughed, we had lunch. I looked at her with awe and wonder. In one of my favorite pictures from that day, she is seated in her car seat ready for the trip home and I am kneeling beside her. What I felt in that moment was a heart bursting with gratitude and joy, and wonder at the beauty of the tiny child who had been entrusted to our care.

Exhausted from the morning's activities, she fell asleep quickly as we drove home. We were all tired as we arrived, so it was an early night for all of us. In the morning, we woke at 7:00

am. I was startled and afraid! Terrified that something had happened to her—what three-month-old baby sleeps through the night?—I jumped out of bed and hurled myself into the bedroom that was next to ours. And there she was, just waking up, a little smile curling up on her face. She slept through the night! She was one of the fortunate ones; she would have well-rested parents.

We soon settled into a relaxed, comfortable routine. In the mornings, we brought her to our bed with her bottle. We snuggled with each other, our little family enjoying the fresh intimacy of our new life. After breakfast, I would give her a bath. I laughed with her as she set up a tidal wave in her little plastic inflatable tub. Later in the morning, she took a short nap, and then we'd take a walk in the neighborhood or run errands.

I loved to go out with her. I'd pack her in her stroller, or load her into the car to shop, run errands, meet friends. Even strangers stopped me on the street to admire my baby. I delighted in the attention the world shows to a new mother with a lovely baby. Was this really me? Was this my life? I had to pinch myself to believe it was real.

After supper, Tom and I would set her up in her infant seat, propped in the middle of our large coffee table, and just watch her as she waved her arms and carried on a conversation with an African violet. 'What did we do before Katherine?' we would ask ourselves, having given ourselves over completely to watching the amazing being who had arrived on the scene.

Day after day, we cared for her. Night after night, we just sat and watched her. She smiled, she cooed, her face lit up. We gave her lots of nicknames: Pumpkin, Baby Bear, Chicken Pie, Katerina, Bundles, Bundle-cha, Bean, Banana, Banana Bean. Our friends stopped over to admire her and share our joy. Our families were delighted that we had finally started a family. Scarcely believing our good fortune, we counted our blessings joyfully.

When I took Katherine to the pediatrician, the doctor

marveled with me at our beautiful child. Tom's mother, a nurse, had worried about her hips, but the doctor said nothing about them and I pooh-poohed my mother-in-law's concerns. I became closer to women I knew through our little church. Young mothers, they now drew me into their circle. All in all, it was great to be a mom. And from where I stood, it seemed that Tom was relishing his new role as Dad.

One day shortly after Katherine arrived, I attended an evening workshop at our church. Tom stayed home with Katherine and I left for a night out with friends. The leader invited us to explore where in our lives we found experiences of the sacred: God's love in our daily lives. We were given three categories: holy place, holy person, holy event. My response was quick and sure. 'My child's crib is a holy place,' I wrote.

One of the other women, a mother of four children from preschool to teenage, teased me in a kind, good-natured way. 'It's pretty clear you're a new mother,' she said with a smile. I felt her share our joy at this new beginning in our family. And over the years, I have never wavered from that understanding. Something about raising Katherine called me to worship, to discover God's love in ways I would not have known or experienced without her.

That summer, Tom afforded me an opportunity I had long desired. I was interested in attending seminary, but that seemed to me like a hurdle I could never cross. Pacific School of Religion in Berkeley, California, offered a month-long summer program. Tom made arrangements to leave his store and to rent our house to colleagues, and the three of us headed west. It was an improbable adventure—but one I now cherish. Tom took care of Katherine during my class hours, strolling around Berkeley with her, or staying with her in our small apartment. I got to study with Howard Thurman and Davie Napier and Linda Clark, while Tom bonded with his daughter. At the beginning of the month, he would hand her to me if she fussed. At the end of the month, he wanted her. He had become confident in his ability to care for her and comfort her.

On the weekends, we wandered together around Berkeley and San Francisco. We enjoyed dinners with a friend Tom knew through bookselling and participated in the summer social life of the seminary. We drove up to Stinson Beach and Muir Woods. One weekend, we took our rental car up to Yosemite and hiked the trails with Katherine on our backs. At the end of that day, we landed in a fifties-style motel room and then headed for the pool. Katherine wore a little white spandex swimsuit that had a pattern of bright, colorful flowers on it. She was happy in the water, cheerfully playing with her young parents. We were in paradise, drunk with sun and our good fortune and our beautiful child. I was as happy at that moment as I have ever been in my life.

We returned to Ann Arbor at the end of the month, and settled into our comfortable, happy life back in Michigan.

In the fall, my friends, Anne and Karla, approached me about forming a play group for our small children. Karla's Esther was a month younger than Katherine, and Anne's son, Andrew, two months older. We set up a routine of three mornings a week. Each mom had the kids for one of the days and then had two mornings for other things. The kids liked being together, and the coffee and tea time at the end of the mornings gave all of us much needed support.

My life was bliss: loving Tom, our precious child, and being held in community with dear friends. What could be better? Katherine was pleasant and easy company. I cared for her, and also read the books I liked to read, sewed, visited with friends, and continued to participate in church committees and activities. I also had a little job, preparing a monthly newsletter for a ministry group. After Katherine was in bed, I would ascend to my attic desk and sift through paperwork.

One evening as I was at my desk poring over the next issue of the newsletter, the phone rang. It was Priscilla, a woman I knew from church.

Chapter Two

Struggling to Breathe

'Glenda, this is Priscilla.' Priscilla was a member of our church, a few years older than me, who worked as a social worker. I knew her from workshops and seminars we had attended together, as well as from regular Sunday morning contact. I was happy to hear her voice, thinking that she had probably called about something related to our little congregation.

'There's something I want to talk with you about,' she began. 'I'm a little worried about Katherine.' The day before, Priscilla had been the attendant in the church nursery and Katherine had been in her charge. But I was puzzled by Priscilla's comment. What was there to worry about?

Katherine was an easy child. She would sit beside a basket of toys and cheerfully stay in one place to play, quietly removing the toys, one at a time, examining each one in turn. She'd shake the rattles and noisemakers and explore the baby dolls or toy trucks. Nursery was fun for Katherine—a different basket loaded with unfamiliar toys would hold her interest easily for the duration of a worship service.

Now here was Priscilla talking to me on the telephone.

'I think you know I'm a school social worker," she said.

I mumbled a hesitant reply. 'Yes.'

'Well, I work at a school for special needs kids.'

There was a moment of silence while I wondered how this information could possibly have anything to do with Katherine. But Priscilla forged on.

'When I came to school today, I went to talk with our physical therapist.'

I continued to respond with little mumbling sounds.

'I told her about how Katherine sits in one place and doesn't move around the room,' Priscilla continued. 'She's nine months old; she should be crawling by now.'

'Oh, I don't think there's anything wrong,' I said, a little defensiveness creeping into my voice. 'After all, kids are all different.'

'That's true,' Priscilla replied. 'Still, at this stage, since she's not moving around on her own yet, the physical therapist said it would be a good idea to have Katherine evaluated.'

I was polite, I think, but when I hung up the phone, I was seething inside. Who did she think she was to find fault with my wonderful baby? Living in Ann Arbor, I had steadfastly resisted the pressure to 'measure' my baby. I had friends who raised the baby in one hand, the developmental psychology book open in the other. I believed that constantly identifying milestones and celebrating precocity could become an unhealthy obsession. Almost in protest, I was less aware than I might have been of whether or not Katherine's development was progressing normally. We took her to her pediatrician regularly, of course. We knew that she was healthy. But I wasn't particularly concerned about when she did what. Besides, though she was born in late December, we got her in April. So we experienced her as a baby younger than she was. She was beautiful and wonderful and that was that.

In hindsight, I can say that I think that what Priscilla did took enormous courage and kindness on her part. At the time, I was angry at the mere suggestion that something was wrong with my beautiful baby. And yet, the very next morning, I made an appointment to see Katherine's pediatrician.

One day later, Katherine and I were in the pediatrician's office meeting with the pediatric nurse practitioner, Sarah. She was relaxed and kind, and with no hesitation made a referral for early December to an orthopedist. When we went to see the orthopedist, he quickly declared that 'there is nothing orthopedically wrong' and referred us to a neurologist. At the time, I felt no worry or concern other than to wonder out loud, 'But what does a neurologist even do?'

It was Baby's First Christmas, so I put my energies into decorating the little brick house we lived in, and preparing for the holidays. This was the first Christmas that Tom and I would not make the Ann Arbor to Chicago to Grand Rapids circuit to visit our parents. Instead, the parents were now grandparents and they were coming to us, because we had the prize. And such a prize she was!

I will never forget the night we set up our Christmas tree. It was, as always, 'the most beautiful tree we have ever had,' and we couldn't wait to show it to Katherine. Late in the evening, after the tree was decorated and the living room was lit only with candles and Christmas tree lights, we couldn't resist showing our baby this wonderful sight. We woke her up and carried our sleepy baby into the living room where the tree glowed in the dark. She opened her mouth with a little gasp of awe. We sat with her for a few minutes and snuggled, listening to Christmas carols on the stereo and watching the lights on the tree.

Katherine's birthday is two days before Christmas, so we combined the Christmas holiday with celebrating her first birthday. Everything was fun that year. One of her gifts was a little toddler bike. We propped her up on it and pushed her around the living room. We snapped photos of her with all the grandparents. She was as happy with the paper as with the presents, happier still to be with her grandmas and grandpas, her mommy and daddy. Katherine was truly the star attraction of the Christmas of 1978. All around her — and us — was a blanket of love and warmth and deep joy.

Early in January, we went to the University Hospital to keep an appointment with the neurologist. When we arrived at the front desk, we were given the information forms to fill out and the clerk told us that we would meet with a social worker following our visit with the doctor. That piece of information was puzzling. We had come to see a neurologist; whatever did we need with a social worker? It just didn't compute, and it didn't fully register. After all, we associated social workers with adoption and scrutiny; we thought we were done with all that.

After what seemed an interminable wait, we were called by the nurse and led down the hall to a sterile little examining room. The room had a window that looked out over the hospital parking lot. Outside the window, we could see the bitterly cold Michigan January weather.

Dr. Rogers entered, followed by one assistant. Somehow, we'd already gotten the word that the doctor had a 'difficult' personality. He was a short, slightly portly man, wearing a professional white coat, with his name stitched in blue over the left pocket. We noticed that his left hand and arm were smaller than his right. He held the arm stiffly, as if he were hiding it. But despite the warnings about his irascible personality, he began the interview with courtesy. After a few cursory questions and a short examination, the neurologist spoke in a slow, deliberate voice.

'Your daughter has cerebral palsy,' he said.

He may have been the most compassionate doctor on earth or a man with no bedside manner. I wouldn't know. I was struggling to breathe.

I thought he had said, *'Your daughter has cerebral palsy,'* but I was sure that could not be true. So she was not walking yet—she was only thirteen months old. She was already vocalizing: she said 'ju' for juice and 'dah' for Daddy and made another sound I always understood as 'I love you.' Anyone could see she was social, brilliant, adorable.

'Cerebral palsy only means "weak brain,"' he continued, as my own fuzzy brain struggled to take in his words. 'It's an umbrella term for any kind of neurological deficit.' He did tell us he thought her disability would be mild, that she would likely 'achieve all motor skills' (translation: be able to walk), and be able to lead an independent life.

We listened in shocked disbelief as the doctor spoke. To us, this was the most beautiful child on God's good green earth. We wondered how anything he was saying could possibly be true. Didn't cerebral palsy mean something really, really serious? What did he mean by 'mild'?

One of the things we described for him was that Katherine appeared to use her left hand more than her right. It wasn't a particularly strong preference, but we noticed it, primarily because I am left-handed. In an oft-repeated family story, my mother loved to tell that from as early as six months of age, I would reach over my right side to pick up a toy with my left hand. She would experiment with me by placing objects just out of reach to see what I would do; I was pretty consistent. I preferred my left. When Katherine seemed to prefer her left hand, we were tickled. 'Oh, look,' we would comment. 'It's just like her mommy.'

'Handedness before eighteen months indicates cerebral palsy,' the doctor said flatly.

Okay, maybe this I could handle. I have weak ankles and I'm not an athletic or even a terribly coordinated specimen. Is this all we were talking about? I started to ask him another question, using my own handedness as a reference point. He dismissed the question. I asked again. 'Do I have mild cerebral palsy? Is this what you're talking about? Being mildly awkward?'

The doctor looked perplexed, as if I was an alien, speaking in an unintelligible language. This time, Tom gave me a dirty look. *Don't go there*, his face seemed to say. Now my confusion turned to anger. I was angry with the doctor for giving this message, and angry that he couldn't understand that my questions were simply my way of trying to figure out what all this meant. I was angrier still with Tom, who seemed to dismiss my efforts to understand what we were being told.

'Cerebral palsy,' the doctor said. 'Disabled.' It would be mild, yes, but Katherine would be disabled.

'What should we do?' we asked. 'What is the best treatment?'

'There is nothing that can be done,' he replied.

We left the hospital, skipping over the social worker visit the university had planned for us. I was still seething with Tom because he had not defended me against the doctor. When we got home we sat at our kitchen table for lunch, relieved when it was time to put Katherine down for her nap, so that we could collapse ourselves. We began to argue with each other until we could reach the place where we could both just weep.

Later in the day, I called my mother to tell her about our appointment. When she asked what she could do, I said, 'Just come,' and she got in her car the next morning and drove straight to my door.

At that same kitchen table, I rehearsed the conversation with the doctor, as my mother patiently listened. We both agreed he was a terrible person. And he had to be wrong. Then we railed against the adoption agency. Why didn't they know? How come they hadn't told us there would be a problem? We reviewed Katherine's whole babyhood. She'd had bronchiolitis about a month before we got her; she was briefly hospitalized. We didn't know anything about her birth or her genetic history.

My mother remembered Katherine had been 'too good' when we first adopted her. She had tolerated the whole morning, the endless passing around, too easily. Tom's mother, herself a nurse, had been concerned early about Katherine's hips. But our doctors hadn't mentioned anything about hips; even the university specialist had given her a clean orthopedic slate. But wasn't Katherine perfect in every way?

Stunned. Numb. Confused. Wounded. Teary. Angry. These are the words that I use now to describe how I felt when we received this news. This was news I was totally unprepared for. Disability was the kind of thing that happens to 'other people.' We lived and breathed in a state of unreality. This surely wasn't true or real. Was it? We had adopted (or so we thought) a 'normal' child. We'd even been asked if we wanted to adopt a 'special needs' child;

we'd quickly declined.

My mother stayed with us a few days, offering us comfort in the face of the brutal news we had received. When she left, we wandered around in a fog of pain, fear, and anger.

What I could not yet fully comprehend was that we had moved from the world of the normal to the world of the broken. It was an invisible line we had crossed, a line that was less a boundary than a full-scale chasm. In the blink of an eye, I landed on the other side of an abyss I hadn't known was there. My friends and their normal children were on one side of an enormous gap, and I was waving at them from a distant shore.

I moved through the winter bewildered by grief. At home with Katherine, any small thing would happen and my eyes would fill with tears. If she dropped a toy, or tumbled over when she was sitting on a blanket, my tears would flow. During her naps I fell into long crying jags.

Tom went to work every day, seemingly normal. Only much later did we discover the slow damage this heartache was doing to his business. We comforted ourselves with the doctor's word *mild*. It will be mild. It will not be severe; it will be *mild*. She will walk, but it might be slow. Day by day, we hung on to that thin shred of hope: mild, it will be mild.

Shortly after we met with Dr. Rogers, we had a follow-up visit with Katherine's regular pediatrician. Prior to Katherine's diagnosis, we had experienced Dr. E. as affirming, positive, upbeat. She was the person who celebrated with us as we welcomed Katherine into our hearts and lives. On this visit, Dr. E. nodded her head soberly. 'You should think about not completing this adoption,' she said, with the full weight of medical authority. Then she went on to tick off all the things that might go wrong in Katherine's future. Pouring out a complete worst-case scenario, the doctor predicted that Katherine would never walk (this in contradiction to what the neurologist had just told us), Katherine would be mentally retarded, she would have behavioral problems, she would drool. We would never have a life; the costs would be astronomical. In short, Katherine would be a relentless and useless burden to us and to society; our lives would be ruined.

This was less than a month after the initial diagnosis. The neurologist had said that Katherine would probably eventually reach all developmental milestones. In hindsight, who knew? Neither the pediatrician nor the neurologist had the whole score. What Dr. E. did was to up the ante. Her message was a frontal attack on all our hopes. At one level, she was right, of course. Many of her horrifying predictions came true. But there was no way we could digest so much of her worst-case scenarios. We were still getting used to the idea that Katherine would face serious difficulties. Now we were handed a platter full of the direst of possible outcomes.

In Dr. E.'s office, my mind just swirled with questions: How long had the doctor known or suspected that Katherine had a disabling condition? Had she known from the get-go? What was she keeping from us? Then what about the adoption agency? Had they known? Was the doctor telling us to give her back? Give her back, my God, how could I turn my back on this baby who had filled my heart with her being? And give her back where? I knew of no 'money-back guarantee' for when the baby you adopted breaks your heart.

But who could we trust? The doctor seemed to think we could return Katherine to some imaginary dead letter office. Would she be able to support us as we cared for this child, or would she always see us as weak, foolish, and easily duped?

As she turned and tsked-tsked out the room I could not tell if she thought we were fools or criminals. Either way, I was covered in shame. Cerebral palsy was new, unfamiliar territory. But shame, I knew. Its familiar discomfort crawled over me now, memories of every missed note on the piano, scolding from a teacher, or threat of a spanking. My husband and I were still stinging from our earlier shame of infertility as a brand declaring: defective, defective, defective! There is something wrong with you. Wrong. Wrong. Wrong. Now having learned that Katherine had cerebral palsy, the burden of our 'wrongness' pounded down on us once again.

But abandoning our daughter at the moment of her deepest need was not an option either. Something unshakeable in both of us rose up, aware that rejecting *her* because of this new label would destroy something in our very souls. We could not, would not, let her go. She was ours, and we would remain with her no matter what.

Chapter Three

God Only Knows

Gradually the news of Katherine's disability leaked out to our family and friends. My friend, Ann, called the afternoon that we visited the neurologist.

'How was it?' she asked.

'Oh, Ann,' I wailed. 'Not good.'

'I'll be right over.'

Ann's house was one street over from ours. The gate at the back of our yard hooked up to her next door neighbor's, so we could travel between each other's homes in a flash. Within five minutes, Ann was at my door, with her gentle presence, and two small children. We got the children settled with some toys and sat down with comforting cups of tea.

'She has a neurological deficit to her motor system,' I intoned. I must have picked up this language from the neurologist. As much a mouthful as that was to say, I found it much easier to recite an obfuscating line of medicalese than to speak the more obvious and scarier truth: 'Katherine has cerebral palsy.'

'Did he say cerebral palsy?' Ann wanted to know.

'Yes.'

Ann is a nurse, a brilliant one at that. She had begun to suspect that Katherine might be disabled—and that it might be cerebral palsy—in the summer, several months earlier. But wisely, kindly, she said nothing to me of her fears. However, every time I had a doctor's visit, she could predict what we were going to hear. Never did she tell us her fears ahead of time, but she was prompt to listen afterwards and to offer her support. Ann was never surprised, but in fact, carried sorrow for us, long before we ourselves could see or face what was happening.

She also understood the medical system and understood quite

plainly that some doctors were jerks, at times research took precedence over patient care, and you had to be always vigilant as you sought the care you needed for your child. Right from the start, Ann offered her understanding to us, as well as her patient listening ear. She was the one who would not let me disguise the truth, yet still upheld me with hope and kindness. She sustained us in ways that I will never fully comprehend. And she loved Katherine. That I knew from our play group. Now as Katherine's needs became apparent, Ann continued to honor and respect our little girl and us.

After the diagnosis, we began the difficult task of telling friends and relatives about her disability. My mother had driven five hours to comfort us the day after we got the news. Tom's parents were equally kind and understanding. Tom's mother remembers something 'not being quite right.' She was troubled that her worries had a basis in fact. We didn't see them right away, but they maintained a kind presence by phone.

Letting the word out among our wider circle of friends and acquaintances was decidedly more difficult. I had spoken to our pastor late in the week of the diagnosis. In response, he continued Sunday's scripture reading—Mark 9, the Transfiguration—to include the passage of Jesus' healing of the epileptic boy. I took that as a kindness, though I could barely concentrate.

In my shock and grief, I became uncomfortable in social situations. I didn't want to talk about the doctor's visit, and I wanted to hide Katherine's diagnosis. I was afraid of the stigma of the words 'cerebral palsy.' I was even more afraid that speaking them out loud would make them real. Maybe if I kept my mouth shut, it would go away!

My brother, Ed, and his wife, Wilma, were living in Rochester, New York. Among their circle of friends was Dr. David Van Dyke, a pediatric neurologist at Strong Hospital. They talked to Dave, and he offered to take a look at Katherine himself. Ed and

Wilma invited us to Rochester. We stayed with them for a few days and took Katherine to see Dr. Van Dyke.

Dr. Van Dyke met us not in the hallowed sanctuary of the clinical exam room, but in his private office. There was a large funny poster on the door with a skier slaloming through a cornfield under the banner, 'Ski Nebraska.' He had just decided to take a position as head of neurology at the University of Nebraska and was looking forward to his next challenge.

Dave was totally charmed by our daughter. He chatted informally with us, and played with Katherine. Then he examined her. His analysis was similar to that of Dr. Rogers: cerebral palsy that is mild. Thereafter, however, we could refer to Dr. Rogers as 'that horrible man' while receiving Dave Van Dyke's message to be positive and hopeful. As in 'maybe it won't be so bad after all.'

His hopeful diagnosis, we'd find out later, turned out to be wrong. Even he—perhaps charmed by our daughter or sympathetic to our feelings—did not see the full extent of her disabilities.

The bottom line, of course, is that *nobody wants* to see disability. Nobody wants children to be born with profound disabilities. Nobody wants to see pain or sorrow. We attempt to fix the situation, deny its seriousness, and barring that, we turn away. Tom and I had already come through infertility. Adoption didn't cure our infertility; it simply allowed two disappointed partners an alternative way to create a family. But to the surrounding community, the 'problem' has been solved. Now we had a new tragedy to face, but this time there were no clear solutions.

So we heard things like 'It's good Katherine went to Tom and Glenda. They'll be able to handle this.' Translation: Thank God it wasn't me! Alternative translation: Don't look to me for help! I'm wiping my hands here. Or, from a family member who is also a pastor: 'I didn't walk until I was three and I'm fine now.' Translation: It's nothing; quit your bellyaching. In some encounters we were placed on pedestals and deified above ordinary mortals. In other scenarios, we were complainers, worrying about nothing. To others, we were simply losers.

One day I opened an envelope that had arrived in our mail. The spidery handwriting suggested that it was an older person writing. It turned out to have been written by the elderly mother of one of our friends. She wrote that she was sad to hear our baby had difficulties. Then she went on to urge us to 'submit to the Lord's will.' Those were fighting words for me! No way, no how was I going to do any submitting! Especially I was not going to submit to any God who might have *intended* my child's disabilities! For more than half an hour, I stomped around our home in a rage. I called Tom at work and told him what she had written. Then, without waiting for him to see the letter, I shredded it into tiny pieces and burned them in the fireplace.

Of course, we did 'submit to the Lord's will,' although that is a phrase I would not choose in my own discipline of faith. We surrendered to the reality of Katherine's disability and cared for her with fierce tenderness. But at the time, I raged! Where was God in all this? Had God *caused* this disability? I was angry at the letter writer, angrier still at God! I raged with Cain: why were Abel's children born perfect? Why was my child singled out for harm?

When I was a new pastor, a young woman approached me right after the service. I was standing at the door of the church as the congregation streamed by with handshakes and quick hugs. Kathy is intellectually handicapped, and at the time, lived in a group home across the street from our church. That morning her Sunday School class had heard the story of Elijah. Elijah prays, calls down fire from heaven, and there is instant, unwavering proof of God's power.

Kathy is pretty high-functioning and uses language well, but because she cannot moderate her voice, her speech sounds like a bullhorn. When she got to the door and shook my hand, she declared in her usual blaring voice, 'What I want to know is *why did God* answer his prayer and *not* mine—!'

Good question, Kathy. Very good question.

Friends and family who learned that our little girl was disabled walked right into that same question. It was a minefield of biblical proportions. We learned that the communities of which we were a part had to make sense of this, as well as we did. Where is God? Why does tragedy happen? These were not our questions alone. And so our friends and family responded often with their own great awkwardness. And often, they responded hurtfully. They responded with: this is a great blessing, this is a great tragedy, this is no big deal, or we have an agenda of our own for you.

I was on the way out the door when my pastor called, several weeks later. I have no idea now where I was going or what I was up to, but Katherine was not with me at the moment, so it is likely that I had an engagement that required I leave her with a babysitter. It was not a good time for me to talk. He wanted to talk then and there and told me it would just take a minute. He wanted to know what the church could do about Katherine. The pastoral care team of the church was concerned about us and was wondering what to do.

'There's nothing to do right now. I don't have time to talk right now,' said I.

'They really want to know what's going on.'

'I don't really want to talk about it yet,' I said.

'Well, they really want to help.'

'We're not ready to make a public announcement about this.' I reiterated my position. It was all I could do to keep myself together; I couldn't bear the thought of becoming the object of congregational pity. This was very soon after Katherine's diagnosis, and I really was not up to sharing information in a public way.

Then he began to push me. 'People are going to get suspicious.

When Katherine is in nursery, they'll want to know what's going on.'

At that point, I sighed and told him I had to leave and couldn't finish the conversation. I just hung up the phone. That was pastoral care. In that moment, it was about how the church could play a starring role in our drama, rather than entering with no agenda other than to be present. The pastor's phone call was more about meeting his need to work with the committee than respecting our need to process our grief at our own pace.

In fairness to the congregation, members of the church later reached out to us in ways that were helpful and kind.

Two of my mother's aunts wrote letters that were kind and encouraging. One weekend that we had been in Chicago, my Great-Aunt Lou showed up in church with a small envelope for me. She had thought we would be in church, but we had already gone back home to Michigan. She gave the note to my mother who simply tossed Aunt Lou's envelope into another, added a stamp and posted it to me. Inside the envelope was a short note and a hundred dollar bill, Aunt Lou's way of offering her support and love for us.

We had one contact we made intentionally, and that was to the agency where we adopted Katherine. We wanted to know anything and everything they had about Katherine's birth and family history. We had been given a page of information when we adopted her; now that information seemed totally inadequate. In response, we were given some more information: she was born after a long, difficult labor. Her initial APGAR score was only two; it increased to eight after five minutes. Ann interpreted that for us. 'Probably Katherine was not breathing at birth,' she told us. There was a suggestion that Katherine's birth father may have used street drugs prior to her conception. Beyond that, they could tell us very little, and the mystery of her diagnosis remained.

The agency eventually helped us secure an adoption subsidy

to help us with the financial aspects of Katherine's care. We still wondered how much they had known or suspected about Katherine's problems. Mentally we see-sawed between bitterness (they must have known) and frustration (they couldn't have known). Also, we imagined what would have happened to her had her problems been known—Katherine would have been at risk for growing up, isolated, in a sterile state institution.

One of the most loving responses we received was a letter from Tom's grandmother. Her second husband's granddaughter had had a baby about the same time that we discovered Katherine's disabilities. That child, too, was born with serious problems (and later died), so Grandma was doubly grieved. And Grandma herself had lost her own first child at birth. She knew well the pain of loving a child that you cannot protect or save. After her loss, Grandma would stand in the window for days and weeks, wondering how she would recover from her own broken heart.

Grandma took her private heartbreak and now turned it toward us as compassion. The letter she wrote to us was written in a style I associate with Dutch grandmothers: stream of consciousness that would rival Faulkner, with the addition of occasional twists in word order. This letter was no different. But then she wrote, 'Why does this happen? Dr says cord around baby's neck. Why does this happen? God only knows.'

God only knows. In those few words, we felt Grandma's affection for us and her stubborn refusal to accept easy answers. We were not alone.

Chapter Four

A Little Shaking in Her Arms

In early April, I observed a strange phenomenon. After a busy day, I was home with Katherine in the late afternoon when she had a little 'spell.' Her eyes rolled back in her head. I looked at her and she didn't see me. I noticed a little shaking in her arms. That lasted about two minutes or so, and then she was fine! It happened again. For a minute or two, she was not conscious and then was back to her normal, although tired self. I was scared and perplexed, but after these two brief episodes, she appeared to be okay. I sat in a rocking chair, and just held her, observing her carefully. She cuddled comfortably in my arms, a tired little bundle of warmth. When Tom arrived home a few minutes later, I reported what I had seen.

By this time, Katherine seemed okay, and it was dinner time, so we decided that we'd wait until after supper, and then give Ann a call. I hadn't yet made anything to eat, so Tom and I decided that supper would be fried chicken from a nearby deli. I left Tom with Katherine and headed down the hill from our house to pick up our meal. We lived on Pontiac Trail, on the north side of Ann Arbor. Down a long, steep hill, and about a mile from our house, Pontiac Trail meets up with Broadway, where there is a shopping center, a grocery store and several little take-out restaurants. After just a few minutes, I had accomplished my mission and was driving back home. When I turned onto Pontiac Trail, I pulled over to the right side of the road to let an ambulance pass by me. *Somebody's in trouble*, I thought. *I hope they'll be okay.*

As I approached our home, I realized that 'somebody' was us! The ambulance was parked in our driveway. Shocked, I slammed on the brakes and parked the car on the street across from our house. Ann was already there. Tom had called her because Katherine had another 'spell' in the few minutes I was gone. By the time Ann arrived, Katherine was going in and out of consciousness, and the spells were getting longer. It was Ann who called the ambulance for us.

The EMTs carried Katherine into the ambulance and laid her on the gurney. I insisted on riding with her, while Tom drove our car with Ann as a passenger. I felt guilty for having left the house for even the few minutes I was gone, and I was terrified for Katherine. What was going on? Would she be alright—?

I sat beside her in the back of the ambulance and spoke into her ear. 'Mommy's here,' I said, over and over again. 'Mommy's here, honey.' Frantic, I wanted to comfort her, and my little mantra was also an attempt to control my own racing heart. Without thinking, I added another prayer: 'Save her life,' I bargained with God, 'and I *will* go to seminary.' Where had that come from?

The ambulance took off for the University Hospital, sirens wailing. I listened in as the driver radioed the emergency department to alert them to our arrival.

We soon found ourselves in a little curtained cubicle, surrounded by doctors and nurses. We learned that her 'little spell' was a seizure. With a seizure, there's not a lot to do—but wait it out. Medical personnel were calm, but took Katherine's condition very seriously. The medical consensus was that the seizures had been triggered by a fever. Sure enough, our baby had an ear infection and she was given an antibiotic. I wondered why it was that she hadn't seemed feverish to me. Was I a terrible mother? They explained that seizures are likely when a fever spikes quickly; the seizure lowers the fever. It's possible not to notice the fever until the seizure hits, and then suddenly, you have a serious situation on your hands.

Seizures are always serious; however, many small children have seizures with fever—'febrile seizures'—and grow up to lead normal lives with no ongoing seizure disorder. For a child with cerebral palsy, seizures complicate the long-term prognosis. We still didn't know this, of course—she was just our sweet baby—and surely when she had been diagnosed they hadn't meant the kind of cerebral palsy that is a life-long disability! But they did. And what the medical staff knew that we didn't is that the presentation of seizures in a child like Katherine can be an indicator that this whole deal is going to be far more serious than you thought. Once you add seizures into the mix there's a much higher incidence of intellectual handicaps as well as physical ones. Once seizures are added, there is a greater likelihood of failure to meet all developmental milestones. It's the kind of complication that may catalyze all the earlier indicators into a significant developmental disability.

After a few hours of checking and rechecking, the doctors decided to admit Katherine to the children's floor for an overnight observation. By this time, the seizures had stopped, but she was tired. A spinal tap had been ordered for her and would be performed as soon as she was on her hospital unit.

Tom stayed with her in the cubicle while they made a room ready for her. I went to the waiting room and sat with Ann. It turned out that Ann had grabbed the box of chicken I had purchased for the supper we never had. She pulled out the box of now-cold chicken and offered it to me. The sight of it turned my stomach. I had no appetite at all. I pushed it away with a grimace.

Ann said quietly, 'It's okay.' Her whole demeanor suggested profound understanding: of course, you're not hungry.

What I was feeling was panic and fear for the well-being of my daughter, and guilt because I was not home when Tom had to call the ambulance. That chicken represented dereliction of duty, beyond its cold staleness and my unsettled stomach.

We settled Katherine into a room. Several young doctors appeared ready to take Katherine for the spinal tap. Tom looked at the young doctors and smiled. Then he asked sweetly, 'And what year are you in medical school?'

That has been Tom's trademark question ever since. Asking courteously, he has found over the years that young doctors usually cough up the truth: third year, first year resident, whatever. He follows up with 'How many times have you performed this procedure—?'

We may have slowed somebody's medical education that night; it was going to be young Dr. Kildare's very first spinal tap. We deferred and waited until somebody with a few more spinal taps under their belt could take on the challenge. Tom stayed with her during the procedure; I didn't want to face it and waited outside the room, grateful that Tom had the heart and stomach to be with her.

Her spinal tap was clear and it was way past time for bed. The children's unit had a padded bench in each room that was long enough for a parent to stretch out and sleep next to their child. We decided that I would stay overnight at the hospital. Tom would sleep at home and relieve me in the morning. I settled in for a long night. To my surprise, both Katherine and I slept quite well, waking only when hospital staff conducted their periodic checks.

The next day was a day of mostly waiting. Tom came to the hospital shortly after breakfast. By then I had talked to several doctors and nurses. Katherine was pretty perky; the antibiotic was doing its healing work. I went home for a few hours to take a shower and relax, while Tom took over at the hospital.

This was early spring, one of the most exquisitely beautiful times of the year in Ann Arbor. As I made my way back to the hospital, I was shocked to discover that life had gone on, in spite of what had happened to us. People were walking down the streets in twos and threes, laughing, enjoying a good time. Some were walking a dog or tossing a Frisbee. Others were rushing to class or heading for cars. Didn't they know? My baby was in the hospital? How was it that the world could continue on its axis when my precious Katherine was ill?

When I returned to the hospital just before noon, Katherine was playful and happy. She didn't appear to be sick at all! The hospital staff had put in an order for the staff neurologist to come to see her, but by seven o'clock that evening he had still not arrived. We all began to give up on his appearance!

Suddenly we realized: it was April 5, 1979, exactly one year since we brought her home from the adoption agency. We begged the hospital staff to let us take her home on April 5, even though we hadn't seen the neurologist.

That may have been a mistake because they let us go only after writing a script for Phenobarbital. Phenobarbital is a powerful anti-convulsant medication. So we began giving her a potent medication with little discussion or understanding of its effects.. I was a little perplexed about why we'd need a medication to prevent seizures, since febrile seizures are relatively common in small children. In fact, I joked that Katherine was hospitalized with an ear infection! Fancy that!

But we happily agreed to the medication without asking too many questions, if it meant taking our sweet child home that evening. We made our way up the hill to our little home, relieved to be back, and happy that Katherine had returned to her usual self.

In fact, life was not going back to our earlier normal. As much as we might like to pretend that 'now everything is alright,' cerebral palsy was *always* on our minds. Slowly, we were coming to realize how much our life—and Katherine's—was changed by her diagnosis.

My birthday is April 18; thirteen days after we sprung Katherine out of the hospital. We did all the usual things: birthday cake, singing 'Happy Birthday,' a few presents and phone calls from my parents and Tom's. But it was a somber birthday. I had just turned twenty-nine. I knew I was ready for motherhood—but caring for a child with a disability—! I didn't think so. I wanted to wake up and find all my hopes and dreams intact. I had deferred graduate education. It had seemed too complicated to get myself to seminary, which had been my dream. Besides, I was eager to be a mom and happy to be at home. I figured there was always later. But things were different now. I wondered what was ahead for me, and was fearful that the life I faced was not at all one that I wanted.

One sunny spring afternoon, Katherine woke up from her nap crying. It must have been a Saturday, because the sun was shining and Tom was home. Usually, Katherine popped up from her naps cheery as you please.

On this day, however, she fussed and cried. Tom and I went into her room together.

'Do you think she has a headache?' I asked Tom.

'Maybe her muscles are bothering her,' he replied.

I concurred: 'I bet she feels the tension in them.'

We were so wrapped up in cerebral palsy as the possible cause of her discomfort that it took us several minutes to realize the actual cause of her unhappiness: a dirty diaper! We cleaned her up and she was happy again. Not everything was about cerebral palsy!

In May, Katherine developed more seizures. These were longer in duration and even scarier. I rushed her to the hospital and once again found myself in one of the tiny ER cubicles. This time, the doctors simply observed her; then they sent us home with an additional anti-convulsant, Dilantin.

The combination of the two drugs, Phenobarbital and Dilantin, may have reduced Katherine's propensity to seizures, but she was now mildly sedated at all times. I was used to strangers admiring my beautiful child whenever I went shopping or ran errands. Now, wherever I would go, I would hear sympathetic strangers cooing at her. 'Oh, that baby is sleepy,' they'd croon. I would clench up inside, feeling deeply frustrated that the medication that was supposed to heal her instead stole so much of her life energy. I knew that she was not tired; she was drugged.

Meanwhile, we were sent off to see the orthopedist again. Dr. Henninger, the same doctor who told us in December that he found 'nothing orthopedically wrong' with her, now diagnosed a sublexed—or partially dislocated—hip. Cerebral palsy can wreak havoc with muscle strength. The tension or spasticity in the muscles of a person with cerebral palsy creates an imbalance that can pull a joint out of whack. Katherine's hip bones were literally being pulled apart. If she were to have any hope of learning to walk, we would need to do something about those hips.

That something was major surgery. Katherine would be hospitalized for a surgery in which the overly strong muscles would be cut and deliberately weakened. Following that, she would be placed in a spica cast—ten pounds of plaster shaped around her waist and down both legs. The cast would hold her hips and muscles in place while they grew into proper alignment.

I had heard about spica casts—and I was horrified. However does one keep a child clean or change a diaper with only a tiny little opening? And how does one carry said child? How will the child play, eat or sleep? The operation was scheduled for August. We began that summer in dread.

One anticipated distraction was a trip I planned with my friends, Ann and Karla. We decided to go away for a single overnight—we chose Toledo, only an hour away. We began planning in early May for a mom's weekend away in early June. We found an inexpensive hotel and arranged for a Friday night and Saturday when all three husbands would be in town and able to pitch in with our kids. The weekend arrived. On Friday, Katherine had seizures that necessitated a trip to the hospital. Tom really did not want me to leave town, and pleaded with me to stay home.

After all the difficulties of the winter and spring, I was losing a day of freedom and fun that I had looked forward to for weeks. There were no more seizures that weekend and Katherine slept away most of Saturday. I was completely disappointed. The let-down was steep, and it would not be the last time I would miss out on something interesting to meet the needs of my daughter. Karla and Ann came back with stories of the fun they'd had, eating out, sleeping late, swimming in the hotel pool, and shopping. For me, it was one more step into deeper isolation.

Katherine continued to be groggy throughout the summer. We have a picture of her from that time. She is sitting in our back yard, in the middle of a colorful quilt. She is playing with a basket of toys, and she is looking up warily at the camera. But her face looks pasty and wasted. I cannot look at it without feeling sadness that our once bouncy, lively, bright-eyed little girl had become so washed out and pale. Clearly the drugs were not effective; she continued to have occasional small seizures, and in between, she was usually tired and ashen.

I considered withholding the medicine, but I knew that withholding prescribed medicine is considered child abuse. Add to that, her adoption was not yet finalized, and I felt a great risk involved. When I talked to her doctors about the grogginess, I found that my concerns were dismissed. It was like it was no big deal to them. She had seizures, she needed this medication, and that was that. I had to give her medicine I didn't believe in; she continued to have seizures and she was groggy. I didn't know what to do about it, except to continue to provide the assigned dosages.

I had a recurring dream in which Katherine was lying dead on a gurney, with a knot of white-coated doctors staring down on her. Finally, one of them speaks. 'We've controlled the seizures perfectly,' he says grandly.

We prepared for the surgery and soldiered on. My parents still owned a big old stroller they had used for my younger brother. At one of our visits to Chicago, we hauled it out of their crawl space and cleaned it up. I bought some foam and made new cushions—this would be Katherine's chariot which would allow her to travel in style after she had to live with her cast.

Two days before the surgery, I took Katherine with me to the grocery store. We had finished our shopping and were ready to pay for the groceries. As I was emptying the cart at the check-out lane, Katherine leaned way over from her seat at the front of the cart, somehow managed to open the egg carton, and helped herself to an egg. This she dropped quickly to the floor. I was flabbergasted by her proficiency and all I could think was, *Good reaching, Katherine! Nice eye–hand coordination, excellent fine-motor control!* We came home with eleven eggs.

If you have to schedule your surgery, July and August are not good times to do it. The hospital is crawling with interns and residents who have just arrived and don't necessarily know what they are doing. One of the newbies took Tom and Katherine into a treatment room so that he could draw her blood. He poked her so many times, she either fainted or had a seizure. Young Dr. Newbie flew out of the room yelling, 'Where's the nurse? Where's the nurse?'

Somehow, Katherine survived the incompetence and came through the surgery with flying colors. She was propped up on pillows and immobilized in plaster when we saw her. Amazingly enough, she was able to sleep; but when she was awake, she was uncomfortable and fussy.

Tom's parents arrived from Grand Rapids the afternoon after surgery. Tom and I were thrilled to see familiar, loving faces, but Katherine could scarcely take them in. Her grandma tried mightily to distract her, but at that moment she was having none of Grandma's attentions. We had planned that all four adults would have a quiet dinner together. With Katherine clearly on edge, I decided to remain at her bedside while Tom and his parents went out to eat.

Soon it was time to prepare our home for her return. The hospital gave us a short course in cast care. I purchased a pile of new pillows for her bed. If we made a pyramid of about six pillows, she could sleep on her tummy in reasonable comfort. I shopped for infant diapers—the only size that would fit in the small opening in her cast. We had already prepared the old stroller—and we used that for mealtimes as well as for walks. It was summer, so she would be able to wear her little dresses. We were set!

We brought her home. Gingerly, we lifted her into the car—I held her on my lap in the back seat for the short ride home. Somehow we managed her care. She began to feel better after the surgery, and adjusted to the cast. We took her for walks around the neighborhood and basically resumed our life. We even managed a weekend trip to Grand Rapids.

After six weeks, at last, it was time to remove the cast. I thought she would be jubilant (I was!), but she was miserable. I learned that a cast provides a secure structure. When it is removed the patient feels unsteady and vulnerable. So we had to wait a few days before she felt comfortable in her own skin again. But we were expecting that she would be able to sit up again, as she did before the surgery. She didn't. We would place her on a quilt to play with her toys and she would topple over.

Meanwhile, it was time for another doctor's visit. The hospital had just engaged a new pediatric neurologist, Dr. Goldstein. Our physicians thought he was both kind and thorough and referred us to his office. We liked him immediately, and he was gentle with Katherine. She responded to him with her eager sociability.

What he had to say to us was deeply puzzling. Throughout the preceding months, we worked on the assumption that Katherine's permanent disabilities would be mild. As hard as it is to hear 'disability' in any form, that she would be on the mild end of the spectrum kept us hopeful.

But Dr. Goldstein reviewed her story. He ordered a blood test to check the medication levels in her bloodstream. On the basis of these tests, he modified her dosages. She was still drowsy more often than I would have liked; however, she was alert more often than she had been. Then Dr. Goldstein listened carefully as we told him of our particular concern that several weeks after removing the cast, she was still not sitting independently.

Then, he looked at us and spoke gently. 'I believe that this will be a very serious disability,' he said.

'Serious? What do you mean "serious"?' we demanded. 'We were told that her disabilities would be mild.'

I don't know, to this day, if he explained himself or not. We were so confounded by this new description of Katherine that we really could not take it in. Instead, throughout the next year, we would ask, over and over again, how it was that doctors could tell us in January and February that her disabilities were mild, and now suddenly they were telling us that Katherine would be severely disabled.

Once again, our world was rocked.

Chapter Five

The Long Haul

What do you do when you get such difficult news? You carry on. You put one foot in front of the other and follow orders from professionals who seem to know what they are doing. At least they appear confident. Since they do not appear to be suffering the way you are, you posit that maybe they know what they are doing. You take the best advice available at the moment and inch forward.

Never mind that most days you are numb inside. Numb is easier than the internal screeching that rails, *Life is hard! I don't want it to be like this! This is NOT what I planned.*

Ready or not, chosen or not, we scheduled appointments with educators and specialists and let them into our lives. Katherine was going to receive early intervention. Now I believe that early intervention for children with disabilities is a very good thing. It's just that it can be very hard to receive.

Helping families learn how to manage a disability is important, valuable work. It is the reason why the hospital schedules appointments with a social worker when a child is suspected of having a disability. Since we had cut out of the appointment that had been scheduled for us, it wasn't until spring that we learned anything at all about the resources that were available to children like Katherine.

Starting the previous spring, several practitioners were sent to our home to evaluate Katherine's needs. In turn we opened our door to an occupational therapist, speech therapist and physical therapist. These were kind, skilled people. Because I was at home with Katherine, it fell to me to manage the meetings, and greet each visitor as they arrived. I want to state again: these were good people. And I hated the whole deal!

Most families build a tight little nest around their babies and small children. Only as the child enters preschool and then elementary school do the doors open wider, gradually admitting more people from outside the family. But this natural process was accelerated for our family because our child had a serious, disabling condition. Our family was opened up to countless professionals and healthcare workers who all have something to say about how you live your life.

When else do people—strangers—come into your home and tell you what is wrong with your child? I was used to family and friends arriving and telling me how adorable she was. That's what I wanted to hear. I didn't want to hear that Katherine had an inadequate parachute response or that she still had infantile reflexes she should have already left behind.

It wasn't news I wanted anyway, but having people I didn't know come over, introduce themselves, and proceed to describe my daughter's infirmities really was very difficult for me. But then, it wasn't about me anymore. It was about Katherine and what we could do to provide her with every opportunity to live and flourish.

After the initial evaluations, we were referred to Rackham School, an early childhood special education program in Ypsilanti, Michigan. That fall, Katherine's program was twice a week, and that meant our participation in our play group came to an end.

Katherine would work with a physical therapist, occupational therapist, and classroom teacher. On Tuesdays, the physical therapist taught us some activities and exercises we could do with her, and then there would be some classroom time with stories and singing and other activities.

Eva Meyer, the PT, was our favorite of all the staff. A wiry, energetic German woman, she was a person who could tell it to you straight, while offering respectful support. She encouraged us to believe that caring for Katherine could be meaningful and joyful, and she modeled that attitude in her own work with our daughter.

'Raising Katherine will be very gratifying,' she announced one day. Another time, she consoled us with 'You do have your hands full.'

In Eva's presence, we felt valued and encouraged. She taught us exercises that we could do at home, and explained how the exercises could be helpful to Katherine.

That was not the case with the rest of the staff. They were a motley group of people trained to work with children with disabilities. Sometimes I noticed small things: the teacher would use a pen to try to capture Katherine's attention on another object. Katherine would always be interested in the *pen*—not what the teacher was really trying to show, and she didn't seem to understand that her own methods were impeding her goal. Sometimes, staff members were wonderfully kind and supportive. Sometimes they pitied us so much, they could barely see or hear us as parents. And sometimes, they were out-and-out incompetent, and it became our job to sort out what worked from what didn't.

Years later, when our son, Mark, was two-and-a-half and Katherine twelve, Tom and I watched from the other side of the kitchen window as Mark stood beside Katherine waiting with her for her bus. He put a ball in her hand, held her hand as he helped her 'pitch' it, and then, when the ball rolled out toward the driveway, with the authoritative voice of a toddler, he praised her: 'Good job, Kaprin. Good job.'

People get master's degrees to learn the 'hand-over-hand' technique Mark had perfected by the wise old age of two. Unfortunately, not all of them had quite as much sense—or compassion—as Mark did!

The occupational therapist was a woman named Shelley. She was actually a quite competent professional, and she helped me understand something about Katherine's upper-arm tremor that was helpful to me (and to Katherine) even years later. Yet, when

Shelley made a 'home visit' and toured our home as we proudly showed her all the things we had made and organized for Katherine's benefit, she found something wrong with virtually everything we had done.

Shortly after Katherine's initial diagnosis, Tom and I, with the help of my father, had begun a year-long adventure in building things. We had read about a practitioner who helped children learn to walk by first teaching them to crawl. For that, he used an inclined plane to coax them into crawling. We built an inclined plane. Katherine didn't sit very well, so to provide support in a shopping cart or stroller, we needed a special strap. I made a big red canvas strap that secured her with thick strips of Velcro. We heard that if a child slept in a hammock, it could reduce the tension in the abdominal muscles. I went downstairs to my sewing machine and stitched up a padded yellow hammock we installed in her crib. In one of the many books we were reading, we found a little table with a half-circle cut-out and a coordinated stool. Consider it made! Add to the list: a carpet-covered cleaned-out oil can with ends removed so that we could twirl her around, a rocking 'vestibular' platform to give her a sense of motion, a scooter board she could use to push herself around the floor, and our favorite: a backyard swing attached to the large old walnut tree in the back yard. The swing had a radius of about thirty feet and Katherine LOVED it. She smiled and squealed whenever we brought her to the back yard.

In her sweet, patronizing voice, Shelley helped us understand how poorly we had done. The hammock was skimming the mattress of Katherine's bed when it should have been at least one-half an inch above the mattress. The table was the wrong height. Even the baby swing we'd installed in our back yard came under fire. It should have been canvas instead of wood! She came into our home with all of her professional authority and proceeded to undermine every one of our attempts to care for Katherine and accommodate her disability! We had made none of these things for praise, but out of our deep love for Katherine and longing for her healing. But the OT's criticisms stung. We never heard a word of recognition that our efforts had use or value—only that we had not perfected our work to her standards.

Fridays at Rackham School were devoted to 'parent group.' The first time I entered the group of strangers, all eyes were on me. The social worker, a woman named Missy, started the meeting by directing me to tell the group what was wrong with my daughter. What an awkward experience that was! I didn't know any of these people and I was expected to immediately— no preparation for me or them—tell them about Katherine. I know I got through, but I also remember how uncomfortable it was for me.

As the group went on, I became more and more uncomfortable. First, there was the matter of Mr. S. Mrs. S. had shared with some of the teachers the difficulties she and her husband were having in their marriage because of their son's disabilities. Mr. S. soon became the example of a father who was not holding up his end of the bargain. Whatever truth there may have been in that assertion, the reality was that he was just a man who was struggling to make sense of his son's disability and make a living at the same time. That such harsh judgments of parents could actually have been harmful was completely lost on Missy Social Worker.

Because Tom was self-employed, he was able occasionally to show up at the daytime programs. I was and remain grateful that Tom participated so thoroughly in Katherine's life. However, when the mostly female staff of the school fawned over Tom and admired him for his participation, I felt discounted. 'What about me?' I wanted to yell. 'What about all the other mothers who get here week after week?'

After I had been attending parent group for a few months, a new mother joined the group. She was black and poor, and had endured an hour and a half bus ride just to get to the program.

She was not a likely candidate for special parent stardom. As she was introduced, the questions immediately began to flow: What was her son's problem? What did she know about the origin of her child's disability?

When she replied, 'Well, I be messing with drugs,' I could feel the condemnation of the group. I thought to myself, *This won't last long*. She showed up only one more time, and then she, too, became new material for 'bad parent' discussions.

Missy considered herself the expert in parents of disabled children. She also believed she was an expert in the facing of grief and loss. She had studied the stages of grief as Elisabeth Kubler-Ross defined them in *Death and Dying*, and used them as an arsenal to reinterpret our experiences in the most negative light. If we happened to be happily enjoying a good day, we were in denial. If we questioned any decision on the part of any member of the staff, we were bargaining. If we were unhappy and expressed any feeling of discouragement, we were so far from 'acceptance' you could wonder about our mental health forever.

She managed to discredit every emotion any of us experienced in the course of caring for our children. She especially could not understand why any of us might not want to be flocking to support group every week.

Missy was full of informative platitudes. 'Take care of yourself first,' she would blithely announce, without deigning to explain how this could actually be accomplished while caring 24/7 for a needy child, making frequent visits to the doctor, maintaining households, keeping our jobs—and now, the added burden of two visits a week to Rackham School. Or, 'It's really good to express your anger directly,' she trilled, going on to explain that she and her husband would 'never have ulcers' because in their home, they engaged in screaming battles in which they 'let it all out.' After Missy enthusiastically shared with us the joy of normal development and her delight in her own amazing and wonderfully precocious two-year-old, I dropped out. I continued to bring Katherine in on Tuesdays, but Tom and I made the decision that we would not continue to allow ourselves to be demeaned by this unsupportive and hostile group.

Gordon, the principal, wore a bad toupee and let it be known that he thought people who adopted special needs kids were fools. (Okay, if we didn't know she was 'special needs' when we adopted her, does that count?) He just thought people were totally clueless and had no idea what they were getting into. (He was right about that; we didn't.) His was an attitude we did not find particularly encouraging. But how is it you can lead a school full of children with various levels of brokenness and be concerned about covering your own bald spot?

In conversation with several other parents, I discovered that we were all 'reinventing the wheel' when it came to building equipment for our children. These parents and I decided we'd compile a booklet of instructions for making the homemade toys and equipment we were using for our children. That was a threat to the system! We heard concerns from the teachers that we might not get it right. The booklet was eventually put together and duplicated, but not without a lot of resistance from the staff. We were only parents, poor saps; what on earth did we know?

The turning point for me came when the occupational therapist wanted to add something called 'oral motor stimulation' to Katherine's daily routine—at our dinner table. The procedure would involve rubbing Katherine's lips and gums prior to eating to help her with lip closure and eating. Suddenly, I put my foot down: there would be no oral motor stimulation at my dinner table! I claimed the right of our family to enjoy dinner without any 'early intervention.' We would just be parents, Katherine a child, and for a few minutes every day, the three of us would be a family together without a crew of critical 'helpers' looking on.

We began to deliberately carve out family time and dedicated ourselves to being Katherine's parents, *not* her therapists. Nevertheless, there were appointments to keep and examinations to be had.

One of our referrals was to Otorhinolaryngology. I practiced saying the word for a week before I took her to the clinic. O- to- ri- no- lar- in- gal- o- je. Repeat. O- to- ri- no- lar- in- gal- o- je. By the time I got to the clinic, I was confident in my ability to say its name.

We got there on a rainy afternoon in late fall. The clinic waiting room was overrun with patients, crowded and noisy. We had to wait almost two hours. Katherine slept in her stroller for some of the time, but the wait was long and arduous. I had to keep coming up with little activities to hold her interest and keep her calm. I read stories; I walked her around the waiting room; I sang quietly to her. Finally we were escorted into an exam room where one of the residents, a Dr. Hot-shot, was going to see us. I pulled a little bottle of juice out of the diaper bag and began to give it to her.

Just as the juice met her lips, Dr. Hot-shot entered the room and ordered me to stop feeding her the bottle! I complied, and by this time, Katherine was so tired, she didn't even whimper. She did fuss when Dr. Hot-shot examined her, shoving his otoscope into her ears.

Dr. Hot-shot was annoyed. 'Is that any way to treat a doctor?' he whined.

I didn't think his behavior was any way to treat a child. After a few questions about her hearing and observing her for about three minutes, Dr. Hot-shot stood up and declared, 'Her aural responses do not appear to be normal.' Then he strode out of the room.

I wept all the way home. I remember driving past Island Park, scene of many happy picnics and walks, and all I could think was cerebral palsy *and* deafness? How on earth were we going to cope with this?

Somehow it had been decided that we should return the following week for an additional test. This time, the waiting room was calm and we were able to get into an exam room in just a few short minutes. We were scheduled to meet with the senior resident, a tall, young woman. She was standing in the doorway of the exam room as we arrived, greeting us with a warm smile as she invited us into the room.

Dr. Senior Resident did not confirm hearing loss, but she did refer us to the hospital speech and language pathologist, Barbara Mathers. The association with Ms. Mathers turned out to be a fruitful one. She recognized Katherine's ongoing efforts at communication—with and without sound—and was encouraging to Katherine and to us.

About a year after the inaccurate assessment of Katherine's supposed hearing loss, I was standing in the living room of the home we had moved to in Rochester, New York. Katherine was in bed in her second-floor bedroom. In a quiet, normal tone, I said to Tom, 'Wouldn't some popcorn taste good right now?'

From the second floor a little voice answered, 'Yeah.'

So much for serious hearing loss.

We did still have orthopedic issues to face. Dr. Henninger prescribed little braces for both legs. We had to shop for little hard-soled baby shoes; then the hospital technician built a little brace for each foot. Each brace had a white leather 'belt' that fastened around her calves, and then steel supports that connected to her shoes. My friend, Ann, found them cute—even as she expressed so much understanding for our losses. But I was devastated. When I saw cute little baby shoes in store windows, my heart would sink. I wanted to put pretty little slippers on Katherine's feet, not the steel leg braces that reminded me that disability was for always.

About this time, I found the book *Journey*, written by Suzanne Massey. Her son, Robert, was born with hemophilia. The book chronicles her journey with Robert—lots of frantic trips to the hospital, and her deep grief and pain. Her words resonated deeply with what I was experiencing. She wrote passionately of her rage and sorrow; all feelings that emerged in the course of the day-to-day care for her child. She also chronicled her family's experiences with various caregivers and helpers. Some were wondrously wise and kind, while others were useless at best and harmful at worst.

But despite all the frustration, confusion and sorrow, we remained on course with the completion of Katherine's adoption. My letters to the adoption agency during that time were full of enthusiasm and optimism. Through the spring and summer we had completed paperwork with the state of Michigan, to obtain an adoption subsidy for Katherine.

A program designed by Judge Steketee of Grand Rapids, adoption subsidy was created to encourage the adoption of special children, by providing for their financial and medical needs, following the completion of the adoption. For Katherine, we would receive both support and medical subsidies. While at that point we were not fully aware of all that she would need, those subsidies made a big difference in our ability to care for her, and to provide for her needs without completely compromising the welfare of our whole family. We felt a growing confidence that we would be able to provide for her needs.

We still had two important things to learn. The first is that care providers come in all shapes and sizes and levels of competency. Some people we would come to admire and respect; others we would find very difficult to work with. We would have to learn how to sort: to make decisions about where and how we would accept services for Katherine. We would also have to make decisions about which advice we would follow and which we would not.

The second lesson was even harder: we were learning that caring for Katherine would not be a sprint, but a marathon. We were in it for the long haul.

Chapter Six

Turning the Corner

When we declared our dinner table an oral-motor-stimulation-free zone, we unconsciously set a new course for our family life. We moved from allowing Katherine's disability to be the only thing in our world, to deliberately carving out some space in our lives that cerebral palsy would not claim or control. Tom and I also made an effort to focus on our own lives, remembering that Katherine was only one of the three (later four) members of our little family.

That fall, Tom and I made the decision to enter marriage counseling because we often found ourselves at odds with each other. We sought the help of Bob and Margaret Blood. Margaret and Bob were sociologists who had written extensively on marriage. Aging hippies, they ran a counseling practice out of their home. Bob was skinny and tall, bald with a stringy edging of long, gray hair. Margaret looked like everybody's grandmother. Every Monday, at five o'clock, we'd leave Katherine with our thirteen-year-old next door neighbor, Ingrid, and head to the Bloods' fifties-style Ann Arbor home.

Seated in their living room, we poured out the woeful tale of our marriage. We didn't understand each other. We had faced infertility and now our baby was disabled. We didn't have enough money. We were clearly incompatible and unsuited for each other. Our lives were a shambles.

Bob and Margaret had a very no-nonsense approach to things. They were very uninterested in our history and far more focused on what was happening in present time. They asked us to sit opposite each other on chairs they set up in front of their couch. Margaret sat on the couch and Bob sat in a chair opposite her. In the middle of this little grouping, they placed a tray table with a portable tape recorder. Each session was taped and then we were supposed to listen together to the tape during the week. We never did that, but under their guidance we did manage to make some changes in how we worked together.

One small change they encouraged was for us to make a list together of our Saturday plans. I had complained that we had done nothing I thought needed doing the previous weekend. Tom said the same thing. It truly had never occurred to either of us that it would be possible to sit down before a tablet of paper and write out a mutual to-do list. To our amazement, this process worked! The next week, when Tom was home, we sat down together, made our list, and were satisfied at the end of the day with our results. This may not seem astonishing to most people, but to us it was a deep revelation!

Tom and I are dreamers. We connect with our inner thoughts and imaginations. We love sharing flights of fancy and floating big ideas. Concrete, actual realities are more difficult for us to navigate, given that we both prefer roaming around in the ether. So getting us to make an actual plan for a particular day and then following through was a significant achievement. Katherine's disability gave us lots of actual, concrete reality to work with: her daily care, medical appointments, contact with the school, and medication. The Bloods had begun their work.

But some of the issues we faced were far more complex and difficult. We were both stung from the grief of our infertility and now the fresh sorrow of Katherine's disabilities. I asked fervently whether God was punishing me with Katherine's problems. Then I would rage—getting really, really, really angry with God because I knew Katherine was innocent. We were swimming in shame over these losses, and the result was intolerable internal emotional chaos and friction that erupted frequently between us. Bob and Margaret gave us this advice: 'Feelings first,' they intoned. 'When you are working on an issue, start by expressing and exploring your feelings. Then, you can make better decisions, because your feelings will have been given their rightful due.' It was a slow process of trial and error, but gradually, we learned some new coping skills.

One sticking point for me was Tom's business. Tom had opened a bookstore in Ann Arbor. I felt that that limited my own choices and opportunities, and often felt trapped in Ann Arbor. I had put aside my dream of attending seminary, except for our jaunt out west and the one course I had taken at a local Catholic seminary. Now with the prospect of endless medical appointments and long-term care thrust upon me, my yearnings and fears surged again and welled up within me.

Shame operated here too. I felt shamed that I had not successfully pursued a career. After all, we lived in Ann Arbor, a university city. Ann Arbor is loaded with ambitious, intelligent people who have plunked themselves down at the University of Michigan to get a degree, to begin a career, to achieve, and to succeed. So it seemed to me like everybody else was productively advancing toward their professional goals—and I was just stuck.

But I was also shamed by wanting to go to *seminary*. The church we had grown up in was quite conservative. While people had begun talking about allowing women to be ordained in our denomination I knew that women's ordination was a long way off. I knew only a handful of women clergy, and only one of them was from the church that was our home. The one woman who had come up through our denominational seminary eventually left and joined another denomination. I knew that another of the hurdles I faced was leaving the comfort of the denomination that was familiar to us, even if we often found ourselves at odds with its theology. Even good friends of mine questioned why I wanted to become a pastor. It was easier to simply turn my anger to Tom and blame him for starting a business in a town without a nearby seminary. The harder thing was to believe that it was indeed possible for me to fulfill this dream.

In one of our first sessions with the Bloods, Tom announced, 'I'm ready to make a change. If Glenda wants to go to seminary, I'll move with her.' I must have dropped my jaw at that moment and wondered if we were really going to need any more sessions. In fact, making a very big change was one of the ways we would cope with all the difficulties we faced with Katherine. We could begin again. We could make big changes of our own choosing. We could start over.

By the next week, I had written to five seminaries to garner catalogs and application forms. We had already made plans to visit Tom's brother, Richard, who lived in New York City. Now I made arrangements to combine our trip to see Richard with a visit to Union Seminary. Linda Clark, whom I had met in California, was teaching at Union at the time and after a tour of the seminary, I met her for lunch. To my chagrin, she was going to be leaving Union the next year. She talked to me about seminary life and offered to write one of my references based on my work with her at Pacific School of Religion.

She listened patiently as I told her about Katherine. 'What a tragedy!' she said simply. I remember being astonished that she didn't jump to 'It's no big deal' or 'You'll be such great parents' as so many others had. In her quiet statement, I felt honored and held.

Katherine, in her own way, had taken down the wall between seminary and me. I had been totally willing to defer my professional aspirations for the work of full-time motherhood. But I realized that I was not going to be able to manage her disability without some space, some accomplishments of my own that did not include Katherine and her problems. I knew now that I couldn't live my life through my child's, and the inner desire to attend seminary made itself known to me, loud and clear. Finally, I was letting go of my internal resistance to facing the challenges I would meet as a seminary student, and later, a pastor. Perhaps it was simply that entering the ministry seemed easier by comparison to total care for a disabled child.

We made one other trip that fall. We went back to Rochester, New York, to visit Ed and Wilma. While there, I visited Colgate-Rochester Divinity School/Bexley Hall/Crozer. Again, I met some of the professors. Dr. Beverly Roberts Gaventa and Rev. Maxine Walaskay spent considerable time with me and encouraged me to come to Colgate. I was particularly excited to meet two such competent women, who were leaders in their fields: Beverly in New Testament studies, and Maxine in pastoral care.

In Rochester, Katherine's disabilities were noticeable in a way they had not been when we visited my brother and sister-in-law the previous winter. We took pictures of the three little kids: Katherine; Christina who was three-and-a-half; and Steve, who was just eight months old. We propped them up on a blanket in their back yard. We put Katherine sitting up next to her cousins, but she toppled over again and again. Christina, for her part, valiantly tried to hold up Katherine, but that really was too tall an order for a child who was still a toddler herself.

Christina asked several times, 'What's wrong with Baby Kahtrin? What's wrong wiff her?'

If it's hard to tell adults what's going on with a child with a disability, it's even harder to tell a child. My brother Ed wanted Christina to be 'polite' and urged her to silence. But I stumbled through a clumsy description of cerebral palsy. Katherine was 'different' from Christina and Steve, and those differences were not going to go away.

Back in Ann Arbor, Bob and Margaret monitored my progress as I filled in the application forms, asked for more recommendations and scheduled my GREs. The seminaries asked for essays in which I was asked about my life experience and my understanding of call. I struggled with this. I wrote about Katherine. I wrote that I asked 'Why me?' fervently and frequently. But I also learned to ask 'Why not me?' Katherine's disabilities had sensitized me to pain that many people carry. I always knew there were children in the world with disabilities. But they were not *mine*. When one of those children was mine, I saw the others in a different light. Vulnerability is part of life as a human being. As much as I didn't like it, I could no longer pretend to be exempt from the human condition.

The 'call' discussion was also a challenge for me to write. So often, when people talked about being 'called by God,' it seemed too lofty for the likes of me or hypocritical to a fault. How could I possibly be called to seminary? Wasn't it enough that I was interested in going?

I think I might have given up at this point, except for the combination of several memories. The first was my practice of signing up as 'pre-sem' when I was an undergraduate student. At the time, I thought it was a hoot. Entering the ministry was the farthest thing from my mind. Not knowing what I wanted to study, I wrote down something I thought was silly and left it at that. Now I sensed that there was something much deeper behind my flippant registration forms, and if there was any joke at all, it was on me!

The second was a well-worn family story. My mother's father, my Grandpa Dekker, had wanted to attend seminary. As the story goes, a family friend had offered to pay his tuition for college and seminary. Because his family lived in grinding poverty, his parents forbade him to go. Instead he was forced to go to work to help provide for their needs. The story was always told with regret, and with recognition that while it might be costly to follow one's dreams, it was far more costly to avoid them.

So I was wrestling with this sense that God was asking me to do something—and still angry with God because of my daughter's disabilities. I was in a conundrum that I could not solve; I could only take one step, and then another, and hope that something good would come out of it.

When I finished filling out all my application forms, we drove to a mail box where I ceremoniously put each of five seminary applications into the mail: one, two, three, four, five! Our family was moving forward.

The Bloods were positive thinkers. We learned later that they were not well thought-of among more conventional Ann Arbor therapists, and we subsequently did more therapy as individuals and as a couple that went deeper into our souls. But what they did for us at that time set us in motion and that was a good thing.

'I have all the time in the world' was one of Margaret's mantras. 'I have everything I need.'

I found the mantras a two-edged sword. On the one hand, they helped me envision positive outcomes and relax into the moment. On the other, they increased my guilt over the deep grief that surged through my life like an underground stream.

One night after a chapel meeting, I sat in a vinyl-clad booth at the back of Miller's Ice Cream parlor with Ann, and our friends Bob and Grace. Located on University Avenue, just around the corner from our little church, it was a great place to get a milk shake or a soda and sit with friends.

'I think I'll need a positive attitude to cope with Katherine,' I said.

Heads around the table nodded.

'But then I feel guilty because I'm so discouraged most of the time.'

There was the dilemma. Was Katherine's whole life and future balanced on my attitudes? How could I have the positive attitude she needed? I was depressed and discouraged most days, worn out and tired. It felt like adding insult to injury to expect that not only would I care for her and her disabilities, I would be happy doing it. And if I didn't, all would be lost. It was a peculiar burden. Some days I'd wonder how I could hold my head up or get through another day. Somehow, I did.

Applying to seminary and focusing on my own dreams and hopes gave me some energy and joy that I could use as I cared for

Katherine. Having something else to do actually gave me more focus and energy for caring for Katherine.

In December, I began work at our local church as a part-time interim pastor while our pastor went on sabbatical. I would be taking care of some administrative responsibilities, organizing the program life of the small congregation, as well as participating in worship leadership on a regular basis. My colleague, Clay, was a seminary graduate and student in the Near Eastern studies program at the university, and we would share the workload as a team, each of us working part-time.

It was a wonderful opportunity for me as I laid plans for my own education, and gave me some small freedom from the relentlessness of care-giving. Our friend, Joan Schaafsma, offered to babysit for Katherine on the two days each week that I would go into the church office. Joan brought Katherine a fresh new face and a warm presence. I had two days each week to leave home and go to work doing things I enjoyed and found fulfilling.

The first year of Katherine's disability, we remained highly optimistic. We held to a kind of 'we can beat this thing' outlook. But after all of the ups and downs that we had faced, turning the corner to the second year of cerebral palsy was much harder. Now we could no longer pretend that cerebral palsy would go away. We knew that we weren't going to wake up some morning and find the world looking as it did before cerebral palsy. We were in this for the long haul, a life-long project. We knew that we had to make some adjustments of our own, besides simply caring for Katherine.

Cerebral palsy entered our lives as a thief. It took our time, our plans, our energy, and Katherine's abilities. But we could not let it have our joy and our dreams. Despite the difficulties, we would resist. I came to believe that as long as we could keep our joy and hope alive, our terrible adversary—the secret injury that took so much of Katherine's life and ours—would not best us.

Chapter Seven

The Same and Different

While Tom and I grieved almost endlessly, Katherine herself was oblivious to our agony. Maybe we hid it well from her. But maybe it was just that we were the ones who projected into the future. We were the ones who could not put our two-year-old on the ground and expect she would stand. We were the ones who noticed that other two-year-olds were scrambling around the house and had learned to say, 'No!' We were the ones who felt trapped by her relentless needs for care, and the endless medical appointments. Katherine, for her part, was just happy to be alive. She tolerated medical appointments with aplomb and enjoyed school and other outings. She was as cute as ever—smiley, pretty and sweet.

She sailed through her second birthday and Christmas with the ease of the family superstar. With Joan working with her two days a week, as well as her Rackham school exercises, she made some small gains. At Christmas time, she was given a small pink big-wheel bike. She was not able to propel it, but with support, she could sit in it and grin for the camera. One day, while we were holding her hands, she actually moved one foot forward in a step, and then another. It was not a huge gain—or one that would last—but it was enough to give us hope.

Life was full that winter: we were taking Katherine to Rackham School on Tuesdays, Tom was working as hard as ever in his shop, and I was enjoying my work for our little church. We continued to take Katherine to follow-up medical appointments so that her progress could be monitored. Our sorrow dogged us. We never could step very far away from the sadness that covered us like a cloud.

Thrown into this mix was a big decision we had to make. I was accepted by all the schools I had applied to and we were going to move. That meant I needed to decide which seminary I would attend. We also had to make plans about Tom's business. Tom began looking to hire a store manager, with the intention that after seminary, we would return to Michigan.

As for seminary, there were two things that we deemed important: one was that I wanted to go to a school where many denominations were represented, since I would not be applying for ordination in the church where I had grown up. I was going to be shopping for a denomination while I attended seminary. The second requirement was that wherever we went, there had to be good resources for Katherine. After a lot of discussion back and forth, Tom and I decided together that I would attend Colgate-Rochester Divinity School in Rochester, New York.

The seminary had offered me some financial aid that was about equal to that of the other schools. That was a plus. Also, we would be near my brother and sister-in-law and we liked the idea of living close to some family members. But the big kicker was that CRDS is located less than a mile from the Al Sigl center, a large building that is home to numerous agencies that serve the needs of persons with disabilities. Katherine would be able to attend a preschool run by the United Cerebral Palsy Association. We had discovered that Rochester is a good community for persons with disabilities, with good resources and a lot of understanding.

Reluctantly, I had crossed several other fine seminaries off my list: Yale, Union, and Chicago Theological. All were seminaries that had accepted me and were willing to give me money to attend, places that I would have dearly loved to attend.

One Sunday night, our guest preacher was a professor from another seminary. When I told him where I would be going to seminary and why, he sneered at my decision. 'Well, I guess if that's how you choose your seminary,' he sniffed, astounded that someone would turn down going to Yale Divinity School, especially for something as trivial as their child's school.

He really wasn't able to get it! I envied him the luxury he had had to attend seminary with complete freedom. But I knew I'd have much more time and peace for study if I wasn't worried about Katherine. My bottom line was going to be to get Katherine what she needed. I knew I wanted her to be close to where I would be. In Chicago we found a wonderful school for her that would have been an hour and a half away from the seminary I would attend. Living in New York City would have been interesting, but very difficult to navigate pushing a stroller and later a wheelchair. What we found about schools for Katherine in New Haven was very discouraging. If I wanted a theological education, and wanted to have actual time to study, it would be important to live in a small enough circumference that I would not be wasting time on a regular commute, nor worried about Katherine's welfare.

In the spring, we were scheduled to meet with Dr. Ralph Gibson, a well-respected child psychologist, for an evaluation of Katherine's mental development. We met in his office on a Tuesday in April during Holy Week. Katherine was 27 months old. Tom and I went together to this exam, and I held Katherine on my lap as Dr. Gibson asked us questions and invited Katherine to listen to a bell, pull pegs out of a peg board and reach for different objects. Katherine enjoyed the experience—she liked being the center of attention, and she was interested in exploring objects she had not seen before, although many of these either found her mouth or landed on the floor.

He asked us about what we observed. We started our list: Katherine was alert, except for the drug-induced drowsiness. Katherine liked to laugh and giggle and play. She liked her bath. She enjoyed music, and loved listening to stories. One of her favorites at the time was a book called *All Aboard the Train*. Tom and I had read the book to Katherine so frequently that we both had committed whole sections of it to memory: 'Round black wheels, turning, clicking. Round black wheels clicking, clacking, turning on the tracks. Whoo! Whoo!' Never mind we were in the office of the well-known, highly regarded child psychologist, Tom and I spontaneously erupted into a sing-song recitation of the book Katherine loved the most: 'Hold on to your hat. Cover your ears. Feel the platform shake.' Meanwhile I was bouncing her on my knees and pretending to hold a hat on her head. Katherine thought we were hilarious.

Dr. Gibson is a very kindly man, and he was gentle with Katherine, and respectful to us. He suggested that her development ranged between eleven and thirteen months of age, and that made sense to us. He also recognized the significance of her lag in neuro-muscular development when evaluating her. He asked if this sounded accurate and we concurred. We ended the interview with a polite and courteous handshake. Tom went back to work and I took Katherine home.

On Friday, our mail came as usual, in the late morning. We had received a letter in the mail from Dr. Gibson. It was the complete typewritten analysis of our meeting. And there, on the bottom of the page, were words I had never heard before, words the psychologist had not used in our meeting: 'trainable mentally impaired.'

Trainable mentally impaired. This was news to me; I felt faint. Once, when talking with her orthopedist, I casually mentioned some information I had gleaned from The Learning Disabilities Association. He nodded, but then said to me, 'Well, it's not clear that she even has a learning disability.' That was as close as we'd come to anything having to do with words like mental impairments or retardation. All along, we had been comforting ourselves with the thought that Katherine's difficulties were *physical* and not *mental*. So this was a shock. And Dr. Gibson had never mentioned mental impairment during our appointment. He had talked about ten-month to thirteen-month development, but it never occurred to me that these descriptions could add up to 'trainable mental impairment.'

I called Tom at work. This was Good Friday, and he closed his shop from noon to three and came home and we wept. Wept for one more dismal diagnosis, wept for one more lost dream, wept for ourselves for the burdens we knew we carried, and wept for Katherine, for all our hopes for her.

If this was Good Friday, then Sunday was Easter. I dreaded the thought of participating in Easter worship and yet I knew I would have to. I called Clay to give him the heads-up about what was happening with Katherine.

With great wisdom and kindness, Clay responded, 'In the last few hours, Katherine has not changed. How you feel about her is different.'

That was the truth. I felt like my daughter had died. We were still caring for Katherine, of course, but now there were still more tears cascading down our faces and a fresh and stinging experience of her 'differentness.' And there was fear, fear that we would never be up to the tasks that were before us.

Then Clay added one more thought: 'You will do what you will do,' he said.

He was giving permission for me to do as much as I could in the worship, or to let more of the service fall to him. Either way, I knew that however much or little I would be able to do in the service, it was going to be alright with him.

Our tears continued to flow throughout the day on Saturday. We wondered about this new information. Katherine's care had just become more complicated. We ached inside, confused about what this new information meant and how it would affect us. Katherine was alert and responsive to us. She seemed to understand much more than she could say. We had hung on to our sense of her as a girl with a bright little mind in a broken body.

Could she participate in the things we thought were important? She loved it when we read her favorite stories—but what about growing up to read novels or history or theology? We loved discussing ideas; would this ever be possible for her? Would we ever be able to include her in our conversations about relationships or medieval history or worship and liturgy? It had been hard enough to accept that her body was damaged; now we were asked to accept that her mind might be damaged too. I wanted the psychologist to be wrong. He knew about mental handicaps, yes, but he didn't know Katherine! Surely as she got older, she'd catch up. She would tell us what was on her mind and all would be revealed. He had to be wrong!

We were having dinner at our house on Easter Sunday, so we went through the motions of preparing the house and cooking. Late in the afternoon, the three of us went to the grocery store with a list of last-minute items. We were already in the check-out line when I remembered one item we'd forgotten to pick up. I left Katherine with Tom in the line and headed off to pick up the neglected item.

As I returned to the front of the store, I stood stock-still. As I looked up, there were Tom and Katherine, laughing at each other, giggling. She was in the shopping cart seat, tied in with the red canvas strap, and Tom was leaning down into her face. They were engaging each other with the love and delight in each other's being that had always been there. Then I closed my eyes and saw the words on Dr. Gibson's report: 'trainable mental impairment.' I looked up again and there they were, Katherine and Tom, my beloved family, simply enjoying each other, sharing a moment of affection and fun. I think I stayed there for a minute or more going back and forth between the scene before my eyes and the words behind my eyes. There were Katherine and Tom as I knew them, engaged in simple play and filled with love for one another. Then the words, 'trainable mentally impaired.' Which one was real? Clay's words came back to me: *'She has not changed; how you feel about her is different.'*

The next day was Easter Sunday. As we always did, we got ourselves dressed and out the door for church. Clay was preaching, and I would read scripture, lead a litany and offer the pastoral prayer. When it came time for the prayer, I stood before the congregation.

'Two years ago, on Easter, we announced to you that we were going to adopt a baby girl. Most of you know that in the last year, we have had many concerns and disappointments in Katherine's life. This week was no exception, as we learned more difficult news about her condition. Some of our personal sorrow will be reflected in the prayer.'

I left it at that and launched into the prayer. I'm not sure how I made it through without falling apart, but I did. A closing hymn, a benediction; we were good to go. There were lots of hugs after the service, but we didn't stay around long since we were having guests for dinner.

Ann and her family were among our dinner guests. I had made ham and—with her four-year-old, Elizabeth, in mind— plain cherry Jell-O. Elizabeth loved the meal and said sweetly, 'I think ham goes very nicely with Jell-O, don't you?' The adults around the table smiled, taking pleasure in Elizabeth's innocent graciousness. The whole meal was peaceful and relaxed. Our friends stayed long enough to help us clean up, and we took advantage of a Sunday afternoon to nap.

When we woke up, we were filled with peace. We looked at each other. This was odd. This was not Tom alone or me alone— but both of us bathed in a peace that took us totally by surprise. We looked at each other in shock, recognizing that we were not alone in this palpable joy. I remember holding out my hands, looking at my arms. Was this still me? What was different? We wondered how on earth it could be that two days after receiving some of the worst news in our lives, we were no longer flooded with tears, but with bliss. We drank in the calm kindness that filled us, our thirsty souls quenched by what we could only name as the Spirit of God.

We might have hoped, after that experience, that the road

would suddenly get easier. It didn't. It did light our path, though, with a sure sense that we were not alone. And as I was preparing—still with some uncertainty—for seminary, this experience of peace encouraged me. Steadily I was being drawn into an understanding that I was called into ministry. Whatever that might mean for me, I knew that we as a family had been blessed by a loving, spiritual presence.

Later that spring, our physician asked me to take Katherine to a gathering of medical and nursing students. They were going to be meeting with Dr. Gibson, and Katherine and I would be the teaching example. This would be an opportunity for the students to ask questions of Dr. Gibson and us.

I dressed Katherine in an outfit I thought was particularly cute. She wore blue denim overall shorts with a long-sleeved red-and-white-striped French terry T-shirt, and the little white brace shoes on her feet and legs. She was happy, and we went at a time of day when she was not tired or drowsy. We met Sarah, our nurse practitioner, outside the room, and she led us to our place at the head of a long table. Katherine and I sat next to Dr. Gibson. Twenty eager faces looked back at us. Katherine knew she was the center of attention and played to the crowd with her sweet grin and jolly laughter. I bounced her on my lap and snuggled her as the meeting began.

Dr. Gibson was kind as he asked me questions about what Katherine was doing and what she was not doing. I was good at finding things I love about my girl and told stories eagerly. I repeated my descriptions of her love of music and stories, that she liked to take walks outdoors or go for a ride in the car. Dr. Gibson was not explaining anything, just asking leading questions and inviting the students to do the same. I knew we were there to study developmental psychology. So I asked, 'When you make a diagnosis, how does it help the child?'

Silence.

I asked again.

No response. Somebody asked an unrelated question and soon we were dismissed. Sarah told me later that the group thought I was 'just a perfect mother' to Katherine. She commented that Katherine was 'very social.' I still didn't get an answer to my question.

That's what we were left with. The questions. The whys. For the medical staff, the diagnosis was an end-point. For us, it was a beginning. We could scarcely imagine how we would care for Katherine. We were uncomfortable with the stigma we now carried as 'parents of a handicapped child' and that Katherine bore as the little 'disabled girl.' We didn't want to be objects of other people's pity. All the same, we needed help. We needed people who knew what a disability was. The diagnosis, though, had to mean something other than stigma. I needed it to be access to treatment and a guide that would help us manage Katherine's care and our own lives.

Over time I would become well versed in 'disability-speak' and be able to toss around jargon with the best of medical professionals. But at this point in the story, my mind went easily to fuzz. I didn't know their language. And my mind was often lost in a fog of pain. How could I take this all in? What was I missing? My mind simply did not work the way I wanted it to. Now when I had all these new things to learn, my brain was failing me, as if it were stuck in neutral between not understanding and not wanting to.

I was uncomfortable with the designation of me as 'just a perfect mother.' I like being admired as much as the next person, but I felt like I was being put on a pedestal, and it was lonely up there. I needed more than a bunch of words on paper. I needed real encouragement, real recognition that the life we had been handed was going to be difficult, but also worthwhile. Some doctors and teachers understand that the whole purpose of their enterprise is to make everyday life better—or at least work. But for others, it becomes an interesting intellectual exercise. What is this? Oh, it's an overly strong reflex. What is that? Oh, it is a seizure. And this other? An athetoid movement. Interesting.

The diagnosis did not help me understand what I really was looking for: what would become of us? We had a new beginning to look forward to, but in other ways, it felt like our lives were over. I had no clue how we were going to manage as Katherine got bigger and fell even farther behind children her own age. We had been devastated at Katherine's initial diagnosis; then rocked again as we learned that her disabilities would be serious, not mild.

We were still struggling to understand Katherine's diagnoses when we learned that Dr. David Van Dyke had moved from Nebraska to Grand Rapids. We decided to seek him out. We had found him to be kind and easy for us to talk to. We also remembered him as one of the doctors who told us in the beginning that Katherine's disabilities would be mild. As much as we hated the 'mild' diagnosis at the beginning, we hated the 'severe' diagnoses even more, so we made an appointment with him, hoping he could help us make sense of our confusion.

Dr. Van Dyke had only arrived in Grand Rapids less than two weeks before we found our way into his schedule. This time, we met in a regular exam room. He greeted us warmly, and interacted with Katherine in a gentle way. We filled him in on the activities and medical history of the previous year, reminding him, of course, that when he had seen her before, he had told us he thought her cerebral palsy was very mild.

We wasted little time getting to the point. Tom began. He said, 'Last year you told us that you thought Katherine's cerebral palsy would be very mild. But here we are a year and a half later, and everybody is saying "severe."'

Dr. Van Dyke hesitated before answering. 'I'm surprised, too,' he said plainly. 'But I did notice that in my original notes I wrote that I had observed dyskinesia.'

Tom and I responded with a duet of 'Huh?' and asked him

what he meant by that. He was thoughtful in responding, and he gave us some better explanations than we'd had before. In reviewing his early notes, he had written 'spastic' and 'dyskinesia.'

Briefly, there are two ways that cerebral palsy can manifest with neuro-muscular symptoms. The first is through spasticity, which simply refers to the tension or tightness of muscles. This was beginning to be more apparent in Katherine; her little fists clenched more tightly and more frequently and sometimes her thumb found itself between her index and middle fingers rather than outside the index finger.

Dr. Van Dyke continued his explanation. 'Dyskinesia is more complicated. It refers to movement in space and can involve tremor, loss of balance and perceptual confusion.'

'But she sat up last year,' I protested. 'And now she has completely lost her sitting balance.'

The doctor couldn't explain precisely why Katherine could once sit independently and now toppled over. He did say that with dyskinesias often comes a loss of balance—Katherine may have had enough balance to manage holding a little body upright, but not enough to balance a larger body. This made sense to me, and yet it didn't make sense. Intellectually, we could sort of grasp it. But it was so against anything I wanted for Katherine that another part of my being totally resisted taking this in.

'Already last year,' he continued, 'I noticed the athetoid movements.'

'What do you mean by "athetoid"?'

'An athethoid movement is one in which the afflicted person moves toward an object indirectly. It's a perceptual problem. The person can't feel exactly where her hand is going and explores a little when reaching for an object.'

We had seen Katherine do this. She might reach for a toy or a cardboard book and her hand would take a little exploratory trip through the air before she actually grasped an object. It was a process of trial and error, as she struggled to find her hand in space and connect it with the object of her interest.

Then Dr. Van Dyke asked us about the seizures. When he had seen her before, she had not yet had seizures. Now he explained that a seizure disorder in a person with cerebral palsy also changes the prognosis. It's an indicator that the brain injury is more serious. We might not like that information, but it was part of what we needed to know.

The bottom line is that the best medical professionals in the world cannot completely predict the future. Nobody notices if a baby doesn't walk—the baby is not supposed to. When the baby reaches a year or a year-and-a-half or two and is still not walking, then we wake up and take a look-see. Over the years, we've also met kids whose parents were given completely bleak diagnoses that turned out to be wrong. 'Your child won't ever walk,' they are told, and then a year later, the child takes off around the living room. Some things can be known and predicted, and others just can't be. I think it's better not to give up your hope prematurely, but losing it with the speed of a glacier is no picnic either.

We told Dave about our planned move to Rochester. Having lived in Rochester himself, he was interested in our plans. He gave us some encouraging news. One of his best students, Dr. Margaret McBride, also a pediatric neurologist, would be coming onto the Strong Hospital staff in the fall. He was excited for us, he said, because she was an excellent clinician and a very kind human being. He warned us not go to Dr. H., the present head of neurology; he thought we would be much better off with Dr. McBride.

While his explanation was the most helpful we had received, it wasn't the one we wanted. Our little girl's problems were going to be life-long and they were going to be severe. That was something we really didn't want to know or believe. We still had not given up wanting her to be normal: to walk, to speak, to grow as every other child.

Chapter Eight

Fire in Her Eyes

Moving was a diversion. For a while, all we could do was to pack boxes and fret about our move. We had found a house to buy that was only a few blocks away from the seminary, and purchased it by telephone and lawyer. We held a big garage sale late in June with the gracious help of Tom's parents.

I finished up my work for our church. The last service we attended was an outdoor service at Island Park. As we sat among friends who had been important to us during our years in Ann Arbor, Katherine made her gentle loving sounds: 'Luh, luh, luh, luh.' Rackham School was shuttered for the summer. We were good to go.

We made our move during the hottest week in July, 1980, loading up a large U-Haul truck to begin our own 'Adventure in Moving.' My parents, who had recently retired, came to help us with the move and with caring for Katherine. The morning after the truck was loaded, we set out in a caravan: we had our little red Plymouth Horizon, my parents' large Chrysler and an overloaded U-Haul truck. Katherine rode in the back seat of my parents' car, since it was the only vehicle with air conditioning. With four drivers, we could take turns at the wheel. Mostly, I drove our red car, and Tom and my dad took turns with the truck, while my mother drove their large, aging Chrysler.

In Ohio, I decided to take a turn driving the truck. This whole move was being made for *me*—and I wanted experience behind the wheel of the unwieldy truck. I sat at the wheel of that complicated machine and tried to keep it on the road. A wine barrel filled with flowers rode in the passenger seat—it had refused to fit anywhere else.

Driving that truck was a metaphor for everything else in my

life! Even as I kept to the speed limit and avoided accidents, I felt totally out of control. It was a great effort to keep that truck on the road as we headed toward our destination. I really wasn't sure I was up to the task.

Alone in the cab of the truck, I began to weep and pray. 'Okay, God,' I declared. 'Are you happy? I'm going to seminary. Now I would like you to please heal my daughter.'

Part of me knew, of course, that it wasn't going to work that way. I wasn't going to be able to bargain myself out of this. I knew going into the ministry was not going to be a panacea for everything else in my life or a talisman against future grief. But that was my prayer. My desire. I wanted Katherine to be healed. I wanted cerebral palsy to be gone forever. Out of my life. And out of Katherine's. I wanted to believe that was possible.

At last we arrived in Rochester. My brother arrived to help us unload the truck and we settled in to paint and clean and fix up our home before fall. I remember this as a lovely time. With few connections in Rochester, we had time together as a family. Our new home was in desperate need of some TLC, so we set about painting or papering every vertical surface. Katherine's small room was treated with a bright wallpaper of thin, irregularly spaced colored stripes against a white background. We rescued a dismal bathroom with a new shower curtain, some pretty wallpaper, a carpet remnant, and with the help of Tom's father, a new set of inexpensive light fixtures. We turned one bedroom into a little study for me with shelves for my books and a place for my desk. I added a paper poster with an ocean scene and the slogan, 'Do not pray for an easy life; pray to be a strong person.' We were on schedule to be finished with our work by the time classes would start.

When we weren't painting or making curtains, we took day trips to explore the beautiful areas around Rochester. Katherine loved the outings. We hiked through Stony Brook Park and Watkins Glen with Katherine hoisted in a backpack. We headed for Naples and enjoyed pie at Bob and Ruth's Restaurant. In between, we took walks through our neighborhood, read stories to Katherine and eased into a new life.

Three weeks after we arrived, Katherine had a seizure. We knew to watch her carefully, and having seen many short seizures, we were initially unconcerned, but this seizure didn't stop. We watched in fear as little bubbles streamed through her lips. Tom and I quickly realized this wasn't something we could handle on our own. We bundled her up, and headed for Strong Hospital Emergency. Tom pulled our car up to the entrance and I hopped out, my unconscious, seizing daughter in my arms. There was no one at the front desk. I stood there, holding Katherine, helpless. A woman in a white coat came to the front desk, and barely glancing at us, sat down and rifled through some files.

'Can you please help us?' I pleaded.

She looked up with a scowl of irritation. 'I don't work at this desk,' she told me. Then she got up, turned and walked away.

I paced around, frantically looking for someone to help. Just as Tom came through the door, a staff member appeared who led us past the paperwork desk to a cubicle. Now that we finally had their attention, we were ably cared for.

This seizure wasn't stopping of its own accord. The medical team decided to give Katherine an inter-muscular dosage of Phenobarbital. That did the trick—Katherine slowly returned to present company. She was clearly tired, worn out from the seizure's effect on her small body. But the treatment worked and she would be fine.

The staff did tell us to make an early appointment with Dr. H., the very doctor that Dave Van Dyke had told us to avoid. We left the hospital, weary and wondering what to do. We wanted her to be seen by a neurologist, but we didn't want to get stuck with a doctor who would be brusque or unsympathetic. Dr. McBride would not begin seeing patients until late September and this was only early August. We called Dave Van Dyke and told him what had happened.

'Can we wait to make the appointment with Dr. McBride?' I asked, laying out the hospital's recommendation.

'By all means,' he replied. He reiterated his concern about Dr. H., and urged us to wait for Dr. McBride.

We called the hospital and got ourselves scheduled into Dr. McBride's first week at the hospital.

Meanwhile, we began to register Katherine for school. The United Cerebral Palsy preschool was located in the Sigl center, which was less than a mile from our new home. Katherine would attend a program there twice a week. We were delighted by the kind welcome we received and felt Katherine would have a good experience in this program.

The next thing to do was schedule a meeting with a new pediatrician. We had gotten a recommendation from Dr. Van Dyke, as well as from the preschool. Because the doctor the school recommended was so close to our home, we started there.

The good doctor examined Katherine and took a medical history. We retold the up-and-down story of the last year, how we had been surprised that Katherine had any disability at all then became confused as the original diagnosis of 'mild cerebral palsy' became 'severe disability.'

Tom asked, 'How would you handle it if you were presented with this situation?'

The doctor's reply was non-committal. He didn't think there would be much of anything he would do.

I looked at Tom, sitting across the little room from me. I noticed that his eyes, like mine, had grown wide in astonishment.

The doctor handed Tom a packet of papers which we would need to fill out to become a new patient in his practice. He shook our hands politely and the examination was over.

As we walked out the door, we shook our heads in disbelief.

Tom said, 'That answer was not the one I wanted to hear.'

I agreed completely. Then I asked him what had become of the paperwork we'd been asked to complete.

'It's in my pocket,' he said, with a sly wink.

He put Katherine into her car seat.

I smiled at him. I couldn't resist tweaking him. 'Passive aggressive!' I said.

Now we moved on to Dr. Larry Nazarian, who came with Dave Van Dyke's recommendation. Tom called Dr. Nazarian's office only to be told that a) he was not himself taking new patients, and that b) when the office did accept patients they only took them from the suburb of Penfield, while we lived in Brighton. Tom did not back down, however. He told the secretary about Dr. Van Dyke's recommendation, and that Katherine was a child with serious disabilities. She agreed to talk with Dr. Nazarian herself to see what he would say. One day later, she called back. Dr. Nazarian was willing to accept Katherine as a patient, and she was calling to schedule an appointment.

Dr. Nazarian's office was located in a small office complex. We walked past a small atrium and found his cramped waiting room. The waiting room had a huge fish tank, always a draw as we waited for Katherine's appointments.

Dr. Nazarian's gentle manner put us at ease immediately. He was gentle with Katherine and had her smiling and laughing with him within seconds of his arrival.

Tom got right to the litmus question.

'How would you respond to the experience we have just had of being told Katherine's disabilities were mild and then almost overnight being told that they are severe?'

Dr. Nazarian ticked off a few things he'd do. He'd talk directly to the neurologist and get some feedback there. He'd want a review of her medications and how well she was eating. He continued in this vein for a few minutes, and then he gave us the answer that sealed the deal.

'Some questions we doctors can't answer,' he said. 'And then we have to be clear about what we don't know. Sometimes we just don't know all the answers.'

So that was it! Doctors didn't answer our questions because they themselves couldn't! We were relieved to have found a doctor who was unafraid to admit he didn't always know the whole score.

Over the years, we found him to be a careful clinician, warm and kind, playful with our kids and serious about keeping them healthy. He supported us as we made difficult decisions and gave us guidance that helped us raise Katherine day to day. He was unafraid to face the truth with us—even when all we could find of it was an absence of answers!

September arrived and I began my classes. During orientation week, there was a picnic for families on the front lawn of the seminary. Tom and Katherine came with me. Katherine spent the time in her orange folding stroller, and we got acquainted with other students and families.

I was going to take three classes: Introduction to the Old Testament, Church History, and Ministry Studies. I dove into my studies eagerly, hungry for the intellectual and spiritual stimulation of being in a seminary. I felt like I had been 'uncorked.' Having bottled up my interests for so long, pursuing them refreshed me like rain. I was delighted to ask questions and have professors respond to me thoughtfully. I began to make new friends and settled into seminary life.

I was out of the loop in some ways: some of my friends were younger than I and single. They had much more time to socialize than I did. Other friends were commuter students. They came from Buffalo, Corning and Syracuse, so were in town only from Tuesday to Thursday. They had weeknights to go out for suppers with each other, while on the weekends, they were gone. But overall, I found a way to fit into the community of the seminary and thrived in this new culture.

Katherine began attending the United Cerebral Palsy preschool on Tuesdays and Thursdays (which corresponded neatly with my class schedule). The program began at nine in the morning and went until 2:30 in the afternoon. Her day would begin with 'Circle Time' in which each of the children were recognized and engaged. During the day, she would receive speech, occupation and physical therapies, all conducted in a child-friendly way. We were impressed that we had found a program that was focused on the children as children first, then on the disabling conditions that impeded their growth. Also, because she was a little bit older, parents were no longer involved on an everyday basis. She would be heading out on her own, spending regular time away from her parents.

With funding from the school districts, transportation to and from the school program was provided. Even though the school was little more than a mile from our home, it was a convenience. However, before it was a convenience, it was uncomfortable for us as parents. Sending a two-and-a-half-year-old on a yellow bus! How could we!

The first day, she rode the bus home. The next day, the bus arrived in the morning and took her off to school. I cried that morning after she left, to see my little one on the little yellow van, but she was happy as you please. To Katherine, this was just going to be one more great adventure.

Tom was still looking for work in Rochester, and maintaining contact with his store in Ann Arbor. Money was tight, but we were optimistic and eager, plunging into our new life with hope.

Late in September, we went to Strong Hospital for our first appointment with Dr. Margaret McBride. We had an early morning appointment and were planning to stop by Ed and Wilma's house for lunch. I remember that because we were sure that with an appointment at 9:00 in the morning, even if we had to wait, we would surely be out by eleven. But at 11:00 am, we had just been led into the examining room. We had waited over two hours just to be seen! This did not bode well. Tom and Katherine and I were tired from the wait and anxiously wondering what was going on.

In the examining room, we had another wait—not nearly as long—but the passage of time was palpable to us. Strong Hospital is a university hospital, so the next person to see us was not the doctor we had come to see, but one of the residents. She took a careful and thorough medical history. Circumstances of Katherine's birth: we told her what little we knew. Age at diagnosis: thirteen months. Onset of seizures: fifteen months. Present medications: Phenobarbital and Dilantin. Then she whisked out of the room telling us the doctor would be in in a minute.

It was more like five or ten minutes but after waiting so long to get into the room and to see the resident physician, it didn't seem terribly long. But we were all tired. Katherine, in particular, was droopy and pale, worn out from a morning of hanging out with two bored, impatient parents.

Then Dr. McBride walked in. She was followed by six young adults in various stages of medical training who pattered after her like obedient puppies. She asked us a few additional medical history questions and then began her exam. She carried a doctor's bag that looked like every other medical bag I'd ever seen, but in hers there were little twirler toys and noisemakers and sparkly things. She used them to find and hold the attention of the children she examined or to distract them while she checked out reflexes.

I raised a concern that Katherine might be having 'petit mal' seizures, minute seizures of thirty seconds or less. When I had raised this concern in Ann Arbor, I had been shot down. 'Children don't have petit mal seizures before three years old,' I was told.

Dr. McBride took my concern seriously. She agreed that petit mal seizures might be contributing to Katherine's drowsiness and she prescribed a relatively new medication for Katherine: Depakene, which would eventually replace both the Dilantin and the Phenobarb. 'Depakene is very helpful for petit mal seizures,' she assured us.

Then she asked if we had anything else we wanted to discuss. I did. 'I see fire in this girl's eyes,' I said firmly. 'And I want to see it burn.'

Dr. McBride looked at me levelly. 'I see it, too,' she said.

My eyes still fill with tears when I remember that moment.

Katherine did well on the Depakene. She quickly became more alert and had more energy. But several months later, I noticed that Katherine was getting drowsy again. I called Dr. McBride and explained what was going on.

'We'll get a blood level,' she replied evenly.

Only if you can remember that so many of my earlier concerns were dismissed by doctors will you understand my reaction to this ordinary medical event. I hung up the phone, sat down on the couch, and bawled. I had been heard! My concerns for my baby girl were being taken seriously.

What we were learning was that doctors are not all the same. A few are incompetent jerks. Some are amazing, even brilliant. But sometimes, even competent doctors were not the doctor we would be able to work with.

We were ecstatic to find both Dr. Nazarian and Dr. McBride. They are wonderful doctors; they exchanged information with each other freely, and they clearly had our daughter's best interests at heart. They treated us with respect as well, and conveyed deep understanding of the ways that one disabled child can affect her whole family.

If it seems like I think these people walk on water, it's because they do. I was beginning to discover a beneficent upside to developmental disability: the amazing people who 'get it,' the wonderful, wonderful people who devote their lives to helping children like Katherine and their parents have better lives. Much later, I asked Tom a simple question: 'Where do you get your hope?'

'From the other people who love her,' he replied. And it was so.

Chapter Nine

Life Expectancy

Our new home was a two-story, late-fifties colonial. Our bedrooms were upstairs and we liked getting Katherine washed and dressed before bringing her down in the morning. Her favorite outfit was a pair of red corduroy overalls that I had made for her. They had a design of trains on the fabric, and I added a little ruffle on each of the straps, which were connected with metal buckles. We called them the train pants. Whenever she wore them, we would sing and chant, 'Here comes the train. Choo-choo. Choo-choo,' as we pulled them up her legs and clasped the buckles.

Katherine loved it! Whatever we sang, whatever little ditties crossed our tongues were okay with her. We developed a new daily routine with Katherine in our new home. Every morning after we got her dressed and carried her downstairs, we had to stop in front of the round mirror in the hallway. As she smiled at herself, it was our job to say, 'Good morning to Katherine.'

I say we had to stop in front of the mirror, because if we ever tried a short cut to the dining room through the living room without stopping at the mirror we heard about it. Fussing would ensue, and Katherine would whine until we made the required stop. 'Unnh, unnh,' she would say, and we knew we had missed something essential. We didn't try it very often! It was a happy moment in the day.

Occasionally, I brought Katherine with me when I popped up to the seminary to check a book out of the library or pick up my mail. She was a little darling among my new friends. The seminary receptionist, Michelle, formed a particular bond with Katherine and greeted her playfully whenever we appeared at the front desk.

So things were going well. Katherine had new doctors and a good school program. I was enjoying seminary. Tom didn't have a job yet, but since he was occasionally hiking back and forth to his business in Ann Arbor as we made this transition, we weren't yet too worried about it.

The next doctor we met was an orthopedist. We felt like this was simply precautionary, one more person in the coterie of professionals that would be available to help us. We went to a physician who was highly regarded by United Cerebral Palsy for his compassion and kindly manner. Indeed, we liked him very much.

What he had to tell us, however, we did not like. He discovered that Katherine's left hip was once again sublexed. We were totally dumbfounded! The course of treatment he proposed was casting her—again in a spica cast—for nine months! We'd been through this before and knew how hard it was. Her previous casting was for six weeks—this would be six times as long. To say that we were shaken would be a gross under-statement.

I think we agreed to meet him again as we staggered out of his office. One issue would be our insurance—we had just signed on with the seminary health plan, although Katherine still had her supplemental aid through Michigan Adoption Subsidy. This was one of the weeks that Tom had to travel back to Michigan; he left the day after that appointment. The next night, Katherine and I were home alone together. Just as I finished putting her to bed for the night, the phone rang. It was Dr. Compassionate.

'I've been thinking about your daughter,' he said, 'and how we might help her.'

What a kind man! Calling me at home after hours.

'We'll have to line up the insurance.'

Okay, so far.

'But before we do this, we should figure out what her life expectancy is going to be.'

I couldn't breathe. Was he saying what I thought he was saying? Did he think Katherine was on a quick course to—death?

He was saying what I thought he was saying. If she was going to die relatively soon, we wouldn't want to waste all that effort on nine months of spica casting. He hung up cordially and wished me a good evening.

There I was, thirty years old, home alone with my baby, and there was no way I could reach the one other person in the world who loved her as much as I did.

I stayed by the phone, shuddering with weeping, and dialed my brother's phone. I was crying so hard, he could barely tell it was me on the other end of the line. Even so, I was bawling so intensely, he could make little sense of what I was saying.

Ed was very tender. 'Glen, I know you're upset, but just try to slow down so you can tell me what happened.'

I took in a large swallow of air, and managed to squeak out enough words so he could get the drift: 'orthopedist,' 'cast,' 'nine months,' 'says she's going to die,' 'Oh, God, Ed, I love her soooo much. I don't want to lose her.' There was more weeping and gnashing of teeth on my end of the phone.

Bless him. He left his own home and drove to mine, remembering to pack along a bottle of wine. He sat with me in our living room, until the shaking and sobbing ceased. Then he poured each of us a glass of wine, which we drank in sorrow. When we had talked enough that I could settle down, Ed went home and I went upstairs to sleep.

When Tom returned, we talked in earnest about what to do next. Katherine's life expectancy was now on the table. She had once sat up independently; now she didn't. She had had a larger 'vocabulary;' now she gurgled and chortled, but had lost some of the words she once used. Were we dealing with cerebral palsy, a singular birth injury? Or were we dealing with something even more fearsome: a progressive, degenerative neurological disease?

In the late summer, Tom had had a conversation with our friend Wayne teBrake. His brother-in-law, Dr. Jim Gage, was working in Connecticut at the Newington Children's Hospital. We contacted Wayne to find out how to contact Dr. Gage. Dr. Gage was expecting our call. He told Tom about a unique program at that institution. A child like Katherine would be hospitalized as an inpatient for a week, for evaluations by all of the hospital's specialists. She could be observed by a neurologist, speech therapist, orthopedist, and social worker. Dr Gage, himself, had done some ground-breaking work with kids with cerebral palsy. They also had a sophisticated video program that correlated video images of the child during an EEG (electro-encephalogram). Following the individual evaluations, the whole team of clinicians would meet together and pool their insights and information. From a team perspective, they would make recommendations to the families for treatment and further care.

Tom called Dr. Gage and explained our situation. He urged us to come to Newington and helped make arrangements for us to come as early as mid-October. I would miss a week of classes, but even so, if this would benefit Katherine, it would be worthwhile. We signed on.

I told all my professors that I would have to be away the third week of October. They were willing to make minor adjustments in my assignments and help me catch up when I returned. When I told Richard Spielman, my church history professor, that I must be away, he responded with a slightly cynical and pompous reply.

'Why *must* you be away?'

I told him, and his tone softened.

'Of course,' he said, 'of course.' He encouraged me and told me not to worry about my assignments.

We were told that Newington was an unusual hospital. At the time, it was dedicated to caring for children with orthopedic or psychiatric needs. It was very child focused, and its professional staff worked in a collegial team-oriented way. As I made telephone arrangements for Katherine's hospitalization, one staffer enthusiastically told me that 'Newington is not really like a hospital; it's just a friendly place where we care for children.'

Off we went. Katherine loved nothing so much as a good adventure. So she was excited to get into the car, our suitcases a tell-tale clue that this was going to be an overnight journey. The six-hour drive was pretty uneventful, and we arrived in Newington in plenty of time to get Katherine settled in.

In 1980, Newington Children's Hospital was a freestanding hospital in a suburb of Hartford, Connecticut. Founded in the late nineteenth-century as the 'Newington Home for Incurables,' it continued its mission of caring for children with developmental disabilities, as well as children with serious psychological and emotional disorders.

We walked in the door and I smelled hospital. *They lied*, I thought to myself, my spirits sinking. *They lied. This really is a hospital.*

We checked in at admitting, filled out a few forms and were ushered up to the floor where Katherine would be seen. The staff were warm and friendly. 'Hi Kathy,' they chimed. 'Hi Katie.'

Tom and I had given Katherine many, many nicknames over the years, but *never* Katie and *never* Kathy. Katherine didn't respond; when she heard somebody refer to either 'Kathy' or 'Katie,' she didn't know who they were talking about! Then they'd turn to me and say something like, 'Hi Mom, welcome to Newington.'

I explained that Katherine knew herself as Katherine, not by any common diminutives. It was harder to explain that I didn't want to be called 'Mom' by anyone who was not my child!

The next morning, we had our first meeting with Dr. Gage. Tall, lanky and intellectual, he greeted us warmly. In fact, he and his wife, Mary, welcomed us to their home and Tom and I took turns sleeping there and sleeping in the hospital. But his analysis mirrored the orthopedist in Rochester. Katherine's hip was, once again, dislocated.

Dr. Gage pioneered something called the 'Gait Lab,' which studies walking for people with cerebral palsy. By connecting electrical stimulation to various muscles while walking through his computer-assisted device, he had achieved a better analysis of which muscles are most affected in a gimpy walk than had previously been understood. He'd had great successes with less seriously impaired children, many of whom he helped to achieve an almost limpless walk.

Katherine would not be able to walk through his Gait Lab, of course, but she could be helped by the knowledge he had gleaned. He did believe that Katherine would need surgery. He wanted to rebuild her hip bone, so that it would more efficiently cradle her femur. The surgery was called a 'varus derotation osteotomy.' I had another set of medical words to learn.

Dr. Gage encouraged us to stay after the evaluation week for Katherine to have the surgery. Drained as we were, we resisted the idea with everything we had, and yet knew we had to stay around for her to have it. She would have a cast again, and of course, that was the worst part of the ordeal. Even when the surgery was over, we knew the follow-up care would be intense.

Every day included an appointment and/or a medical test of some kind. We met a Dr. Russman, a neurologist, who listened patiently as we poured out the puzzle of the last year. We knew we had heard words when Katherine was about a year old, some words we no longer heard. We were still frustrated that she had had sitting balance and lost it. We didn't really believe she was mentally handicapped, only physically impaired. We recounted the whole emotional tale.

Dr. Russman told us several things that were helpful to us. He suggested that Katherine could be a 'locked-in' child. That is, whatever is going on in Katherine's mind could be locked inside her, prevented from expression because of the severity of her physical handicaps. That has stayed with me over the years; I have usually erred in the direction of telling Katherine more than she may understand. We didn't know what Katherine understood; we were not going to ever hold information or learning back from her. So whether it was reading stories, or going to the zoo, or visiting the doctor, we talked to her about what was going on, wanting to give her as much information as her brain could accept.

In the end, he, too, affirmed the diagnosis of cerebral palsy — a singular birth injury, rather than a more pernicious degenerative disorder. The life expectancy issues were off the table, and we were told to expect that she would grow to adulthood.

The week was a roller-coaster. We put on our 'intelligent thoughtful parent' faces as much as possible, but it was difficult to hide from the painful feelings that were roiling inside us. On Tuesday night, we waited until Katherine was asleep for the night, then we slipped out of the hospital so we could eat regular food at a local restaurant. After we had been served, the waitress returned to our table to cheerfully ask, 'Is everything okay here?'

Tom managed a pleasant, appropriate response: 'Yes, we're fine,' but the minute the waitress turned her back, tears spilled out of my eyes.

'No, everything is NOT okay,' I fumed. 'My baby is in the hospital and it feels like the whole world is falling apart.'

Tom reached across the table for my hand, and held it gently. We sat with our pain and swallowed down our supper before returning to the hospital.

On Thursday, we were sent to Hartford Hospital, so that Katherine could have a CT scan of her head. We were driven to the other hospital in a hospital van and let off by the front door. We found the location for the scan and sat to wait. The first thing the staff did was to give Katherine an injection of a sedative so that she would be relaxed and comfortable as the scanner — an early model CT scanner which was a noisy, metal, circular machine—spun around her head. As she began to relax, the staff urged us to go to the cafeteria for something to eat and drink.

'You need a break,' they urged. 'And she'll be fine.'

After being assured that they would not start the test until we returned, we left and headed for the cafeteria. When we came back, less than twenty minutes later, we discovered that Katherine had already been placed in the CT scanner. We had been lied to!

As we waited in the hallway, a nurse came out of the room where Katherine lay. She had just given Katherine another shot of the sedative, she told us, because Katherine started to wake up in the scanner. Her manner was jovial, as if poking my daughter in her hand was sort of funny. But to me, it was a moment of intense anguish. Katherine was a child who never kept a hat on. Put one on her head, it flew off in a minute. To see her alone, with this loud metal machine revolving around her precious head, then waking, then getting stuck again with a needle was way more than I could bear.

We had been labeled 'overprotective' parents because we rarely left her alone when she was in the hospital. Why would we? Katherine could not speak, but we could understand if she was uncomfortable or unhappy or in need. We could comfort her. While we cooperated with hospital staff, we always asked lots of questions and tried to understand what we were being told. Now we were also being blamed for our devotion to our daughter, and tricked into abandoning her. I'm sure hospital personnel never understood how making their job easier for themselves had just ratcheted up our pain to turbo levels.

They sprung Katherine from the hospital for the weekend. The tests and evaluations were complete and she was scheduled for surgery the following Monday, but there was no reason we had to hang around Friday afternoon, Saturday or Sunday morning. We escaped to Mystic, Connecticut, because we heard that the seaport was very beautiful. Unfortunately, we landed in Mystic during a driving rain storm and had to spend most of our time languishing in a cheap hotel.

The surgery happened on schedule. In the waiting area, I sat for a while near a mother whose son was having a minor eye surgery. As she described it, he would probably make a full recovery and lead a totally normal life. Then she described how hard it had been for her to accept this surgery. She told me that she finally realized, 'God never gives you more burdens than you can bear.'

There is no phrase that I find more hurtful. I know some people find comfort in those words, but I want to jump out of my skin when somebody tries that phrase out on me. I believe that I remained polite, and made an effort at emotional control as I told her I absolutely did not agree. If God gets specific blame for every tragedy, then where is God when the need is great? I surely wouldn't be seeking comfort from the very source of my pain. And furthermore, human beings break. Sometimes under the strain of intolerable burdens, people don't make it. They fall apart, as I was getting close to doing right then and there.

When Katherine came out of surgery, her color was good, but once again she was buried in plaster. One thing was different from the earlier experience of casting: the Newington staff really understood cast care. First, they layered her bed with a 'U-board,' a homemade platform shaped like a 'U.' Katherine's torso fit on the solid part of the board, and her legs fit on the sides of the U. A bedpan could be placed in the opening, so that the cast could be kept clean and Katherine as comfortable as possible. I learned from the nursing staff how to 'petal' the cast: using soft, adhesive moleskin, we cut little rounded patches—petals—that we placed all around the edges of the cast. The petals softened the cast where it touched Katherine's skin, and could be changed when they became soiled.

We often were helped by a man named Freddy. One of the orderlies, he was responsible for transporting patients to laboratory tests or appointments. He had grown up as a child when Newington was still a 'Home for Incurables.' He seemed as comfortable with his place in the world as anyone. He knew the hospital upside and down. In his own quiet way, he provided comfort, and he could be counted on to find a rocking chair when one was needed with as much ease as he offered directions to the cafeteria.

One breath of great fresh air in all this was that we were often visited by Dr. Gage's wife, Mary. In the afternoons while Katherine recovered from surgery she would appear with her kind spirit and gentleness. One of those afternoons, I took advantage of her presence to walk down the street to a nearby drug and gift store. I purchased for myself a beautiful dark brown coffee mug and brought it, smiling, back to the hospital. I had so little control while I was with Katherine—but they could not make me drink my tea in Styrofoam. I was now equipped with a real ceramic mug.

We returned to Rochester, with Katherine carefully cradled in the back seat. The trip was uneventful. Her preschool was prepared to accept her, cast and all.

But it was almost November and it was cold in Rochester. She would need something more than a dress and bare legs. To get her ready for school, I got out my sewing machine once again. This time, the overalls I made were two sizes larger than she would normally wear, but I made them with a snap-crotch, so that they would fit around her cast. Gussied up in her new outfits, off she went, and we were in business again.

Once Katherine went back to school, I could go back to school myself. Katherine's second week in the hospital was my reading week, so I had missed only one week of classes. After a little deliberation, I chose to drop one of my classes and concentrate on the two that were left, a strategy that served me well. I was happy to be back on 'my own turf,' and to reconnect with my new friends.

There was one little problem, however. Seminaries are filled with pastor wannabes, so I was quickly on the receiving end of way too much pastoral care and attempted active listening. I finally took to avoiding the seminary with all the watchful, compassionate eyes boring into me, and went only for classes and to take books out of the library. I did my studying at home for a while; until my classmates lost interest in our problem and went on to try out their new skills on others.

Also, I myself became very impatient with other students. There is a lot of highly intellectualized kvetching and whining that goes on in seminaries—I had very little tolerance for any of it. I just felt my problems were the worst in the world. It was another reason that put a little distance between me and seminary life.

Tom had to return to Ann Arbor—this visit would be for a week, so my mother offered to spend the time with Katherine and me. It was now clear that replacing Tom with a manager at his bookshop was not working out very well. Tom was shaken by our experiences at Newington, as well as by the diminished condition of his shop. I was angry, because we were now in very dangerous financial straits. The little nest egg that was tiding us over was next to nothing. Though it was not in our plans originally, I took out a loan to help with expenses. So it was a tough time. For me, the best part of the season was that I was studying as I had hoped to, and could lose myself in the books I read and papers I wrote.

Katherine was scheduled to return to Newington in December so that her cast could be removed. She had had pins placed in her hip and these would be removed in a brief surgery. There was only one problem: a scheduling conflict between my exams and Katherine's appointments.

Tom bravely offered to drive her to Newington by himself. I stayed behind and passed my tests. We were looking forward to a Christmas season with no cast. However, Dr. Gage determined that her hip was not healed as well as he wanted; he put a new, small cast on her thighs with a bar in between to hold her hips in position. It was an easier cast to manage, but a cast is a cast is a cast. It was still plaster in an uncomfortable place.

Because it was Christmas time, the halls of Newington had been filled with generous carolers and donors. Katherine was given so many toys and games, they filled a coffin-sized box. Most of the toys were not even suitable for Katherine, because she would not be able to manipulate them. We gave most of them to Katherine's cousins, Steve and Christina, who were then two and four.

Christina's eyes were wide with amazement when she witnessed this largesse. 'I wish I could go the hospital,' she said.

We came to Christmas weary and lost. We were broke—financially far more fragile than we had planned. Katherine had come through yet another surgery. I had made new friends, but we did not have a lot of time to fully enjoy the seminary community. We were glum, short with each other and not very good company.

In spite of our crabbiness, we did purchase a tree and set it up, a pro-forma activity. We argued as we put the tree in its stand. 'Can't you work faster?' 'The tree is crooked.' 'I'm working as fast as I can.'

We put up the lights with a similar lack of cordiality. Then we whipped out the ornament box and something changed.

There was the little manger ornament that we'd bought in Ann Arbor the second year we were married. I found the ugly plastic twirler that had been on our tree when I was a child, and the large colored light bulbs that produced enough heat to make it spin. I added the metal Star of David ornament that I had been given by a new friend. On and on it went. We had shared some very good memories. We also wanted a future together. As we sorted through the ornaments, we remembered these things.

We found a peaceful place once again. In spite of all we'd been through, and all the words and harsh feelings that we passed to each other, we were granted this one moment when Christmas gave us a glimpse of serenity and hope.

Chapter Ten

Chilled

Rochester, New York, has a well-deserved reputation for cold and snowy winters. What is less well known is that even a snowfall of two feet does not bring things to a halt. Tom and I are Midwest natives and no strangers to cold and snow, but we were shocked the first time a snowstorm dropped over a foot of snow on our region and nothing stopped. In Rochester, whenever it snows, the plows roll out; they pick up the snow, move it over, or dump it in the Genesee River, and unless there are white-out conditions, you don't get to skip school. You put on a jacket, pull on your boots and go out.

Katherine had turned three late in that cold December. The lag between her development and that of other children her age was now visible and undeniable—and growing more difficult for us. She wasn't talking. She could not crawl, sit, or stand. She needed us to dress her, feed her and change her diaper. Caring for her was like caring for a helpless infant, except this 'infant' weighed more. Carrying her became more difficult, even when she wasn't sporting a few pounds of plaster on her legs and around her hips. Not only was her size a factor; she did not move with the fluidity of a normal child. She could not 'cling' to us as we carried her, wrapping her little body around ours. She could not move her foot or arm out of the way of a door jamb, for example. She could not support her weight on her feet even for a moment.

Early in her life, her care was easier than most babies' because she was so cheerful, and she couldn't get into mischief. Now, though we did not hear the 'no' that parents dread, and we rarely saw tantrums, her daily care intensified, as she grew larger and we grew weary of the total care we had to provide a child who— had she not had a disability—would have been toddling around.

In February, her small cast was removed. We found a doctor in Rochester, Dr. Robert Schrock, who was interested in the work of Dr. Gage, and was happy to treat Katherine, working in cooperation with Dr. Gage. It took me until March or April until all the paperwork for her hospitalizations cleared and I had dispensed with the clerical obligations that are an often unrecognized follow-up to any experience with medical care.

Katherine was now in school five days a week, and that made the rest of our lives easier to manage. It meant I had five days a week to attend classes and to study. We had to work hard to keep up our schedules, but we were able to manage. When she was home with us, we had to focus on her; she required that we provide total care for everything she needed.

What she could do was charm us and that she did in spades. At an age when most little people are exploring their world, she was content with lying in place on a quilt and playing with her infant toys. She liked listening to music and she was delighted when we read stories to her or simply held her. On a cold winter's night, we sat together, rocking in front of a warm fire. Cuddled in my arms, she warmed me as much as I did her.

Indeed the chill that was coming over me was less because of the cold Rochester winter, than the emerging failure of Tom's store in Michigan. I knew I wasn't getting the whole story when creditors began calling our home and demanding money. I was nonplussed. I had had no idea that Tom's company was in arrears, or how much money was needed. I tried to explain to the hostile voices on the phone that I had no responsibility for his business, that I was not the one they needed to talk with.

They were not put off. They were rude and hostile and reminded me that as his wife, I could be held legally liable for his debts. I was shocked and enraged, ready to throttle Tom every time I looked at him. Except for Katherine, our home became an armed camp. In her presence, we tried to tamp down our rage and protect her. But there was no denying that Tom and I were not in a good place with each other. He had not kept me fully informed about his business decisions and losses; I felt betrayed to be learning of the damage through harassing bill collectors. I was afraid financially, and I was afraid for our family.

Our home life was tense and strained. Life at the seminary became my refuge. My friendships were becoming richer— although I held inside most of the fear and pain of our family life. My classes engaged me. I liked the stimulating discussions that are part of seminary life and reveled in the new opportunities that were presented to me.

One opportunity was an extra-curricular class on meditation. It was held at a local Presbyterian church and led by a therapist who had come to the seminary for a year as a non-degree student. In my family, prayer meant the beginning and end of dinner time. It was a fairly formal event, with occasional references to blessing the sick, and my father's petition when he faced difficulties at work: 'Grant that our efforts might be met with success.'

Despite assurances to the contrary, I did not really believe in praying for outcomes. I saw little evidence for its usefulness. Nice people I knew spoke about the 'power of prayer,' but it didn't register with me. I prayed, but if pushed, I would have had to say I thought it was pretty naïve for people to think that if you prayed, cancer would be healed, divorcing partners would like each other again, or rain would fall. But since Katherine's disability, formal prayer did not serve me. I called out to the heavens with my profound longing and anguish and found little relief.

Meditation was a new avenue. Sitting in silence, quietly listening to my own breath, and mentally repeating 'Be still and know,' opened me to a new dimension of prayer. To be sure, these were baby steps, but I was learning, slowly, to find a place in myself where God was present.

Classes in New Testament and Ministry Studies gave me loads of excuses to explore the meaning of Katherine's disability in a disciplined way. I shamelessly exploited my own stories of raising a disabled child to garner good grades. Seminary faculty want students who do not shy away from human difficulty, so when I wrote passionately about discovering that Katherine was mentally impaired, or about waiting for Katherine as she endured her CT scan, my work was evaluated highly.

When it was time to write a formal paper on a New Testament text, I chose to work with a story of one of Jesus' healing miracles. I was able to come to the conclusion that the task of faith was not to create a miracle, but to recognize it when it comes. I wrote,

Now I will let go a little, lose a little of my scholarly restraint. My daughter is crippled, my own child. For two years I have been railing at God: 'Do something! Don't I believe enough? Haven't I prayed enough?'

I see 'miracles' in the gospels and I yell, 'Well, if you could do it then, do it now!' The stories multiplied my anguish. I thought they were stories about making miracles.

Then I read them. And I found that the story is about faith: human faith in the midst of crisis, human faith in the power of God.

I concluded by mentioning the way Jesus touches those who long to be healed, not with the critical examination of the clinician, but with a caress of love.

Thriving in my studies, I felt like I was dying in my home. In March, Tom went back to Ann Arbor for a week. The situation was now completely desperate. The manager Tom had hired was understandably angry with Tom that the business was so unstable. At the same time, he did not always follow Tom's directions and advice. Finally, Tom worked out a deal with him that basically left him with the business and Tom with the debts. Meanwhile, I was in Rochester, alone, caring for Katherine and wondering how I would make it to the end of the semester, much less all the way through school.

No, my fears were deeper than that. I was beginning to think seriously about leaving Tom. And I was wondering about my own survival—and Katherine's. How was I going to make it in the world? How was I going to provide for myself and Katherine—or even care for her on my own?

I made an appointment to speak with my professor of pastoral care, Dr. Maxine Walaskay. She invited me into her office, and quietly shut the door. We sat, and I poured out my whole story.

Maxine looked across the small room and said levelly, 'It sounds like your whole life is up for grabs.'

I heaved a deep sigh and let my tears seep out of my eyes.

She continued, 'Your marriage is in deep trouble, you are running out of money, you may have to drop out of school, and you may have to move.'

I was learning about pastoral care from the inside out. Her acknowledgement of my agony was a relief even if what she did was to lay out the severity of our situation for my viewing. She didn't offer any solutions; she simply gave the reassurance of a presence that did not look away from my distress.

I could not see the future; I didn't know how I would make it. My trust in Tom had been thoroughly shattered by the business losses. I felt alone in the world and could not figure out how I would move forward.

In desperation, I called my brother, and asked to meet at his office. 'I have decided that I will divorce Tom,' I said, when we met. He nodded. He was not surprised. I made a stop in the Dean of Students office and asked about the availability of on-campus student housing. Bill Bross, who handled financial aid, winced as he listened to me. 'Not you, too,' he said.

Seminary divorces, unfortunately, were increasingly common. It seemed that as one partner in the marriage—the seminarian— was growing and changing, the other partner was frequently befuddled by the changes or left in the dust. Now we were also on the precipitous brink. In our case, it was less about seminary than all the staggering losses that buffeted our lives. Tom was quite supportive of my education. The one thing that helped us was that we *didn't* live on campus and could keep our problems out of general sight and away from the gossips. So this was all swirling around at once. I liked my studies and the friends I was making at school. But our family foundation was crumbling.

One of our seminary assignments was to meet at least three times with a pastoral counselor. We were expected to learn what it feels like to begin a counseling relationship and write about our experiences. I made an appointment with Marie Johnson, who met me on the seminary campus.

Marie is a petite woman with sharp features and a huge, warm heart. She is also incisive, deliberate, and unfailingly direct. We began to meet—and continued on well past the course requirement. After listening to me drone on and on about all my problems, she stopped me one day and said, 'You're telling me what you think. What do you feel?'

I really did not know how to answer that question. My emotions were attached to a spin cycle that was whirling around in my head. Mentally, I regurgitated tales of abandonment, disappointment, betrayal—all of it a repetitious recounting of blame.

Marie pressed on. 'You're talking from your head. What does it feel like in here?' she asked, patting her own belly and pointing to mine.

My façade was beginning to crumble. It felt awful. My self-talk helped me to keep the fierce pain and rage hidden from full recognition. I didn't want to feel these things, but I was dying inside and Marie knew it.

That weekend, while Tom was still away, I finished one of my papers. Because the seminary was closed that Saturday afternoon, the only place I could make the copies I needed was at the Brighton Public Library. I packed Katherine up into the car, put my paper in a cardboard file, and drove the short distance to the library. As we got out of the car, Katherine chortled with glee. She recognized the library!

'Are you happy to be here, Katherine?' I asked.

Happy noises.

'And you want to read stories.'

'Ya-eh.'

'This is where Daddy takes you.'

Laughter.

She recognized the library because her father had frequently taken her there. He had taken it upon himself to take her to the library and check out storybooks. He would pull books off shelves and let her see the different titles. Then the two of them would make their choices and carry home four or five children's titles.

Something hard inside of me softened. This man who was the focus of so much of my rage brought his severely disabled three-year-old daughter to the public library to read stories. Once again I was standing in the middle of a paradox: my husband had lost a great deal of money in a business he had mismanaged, had lied to me outright and by dissembling about the situation. These were behaviors I could neither accept nor tolerate. He also read to his severely disabled three-year-old daughter, and took her to the library to collect interesting books.

Much later, we were able to trace the beginning of the decline of his business to January, 1979, the very month that Katherine was diagnosed. At the time, it looked like I was the messed-up one: home with Katherine, I cried at every turn. But Tom went off to work, looking like he was holding it together, only to lose his grip as the company he once led so ably slipped from his grasp.

I wish I could say that everything was fine and dandy after the insight in the library. It wasn't. What did happen is that we sought counseling as a couple again, and I continued my individual work with Marie. Slowly we worked to rebuild trust. It was a very slow process; I now believe that the unbearable grief we faced, combined with our own immaturity and weakness, set us up for near disaster. Sometimes facing disability made us crabby, irritable, and unpleasant. In addition, we brought our previously shaky financial record, and our limited ability to express ourselves clearly and kindly. All our personal limitations and idiosyncratic foibles were magnified by the challenges we faced with Katherine.

Our home had become a place that Tom and I took turns leaving. It was a place where we felt our losses. Tom found a job at an insurance company. I had my seminary education. Together we had Katherine, whom we both loved fiercely. We also felt burdened and weary because of her deep needs and distant from each other. We had lots of work to do, and the dance we took with each other was often clumsy and awkward.

Bob and Margaret Blood had urged us on like high school cheerleaders: go team, go team, go! To sustain our momentum, we had to go much deeper into our souls.

Chapter Eleven

Second Year

I started my second year of seminary eagerly. I was freed from the first-year fears of academic inadequacy, and did not yet have to face leaving the safety of the seminary for the reality of finding work in a parish. Coming back in after a summer break, I was happy to see my friends again and dig into my coursework.

I did my field education that year, assigned to Mountain Rise United Church of Christ, in Fairport, New York. It was an opportunity to learn how to be a pastor. Rev. Karl Johnson was my supervisor. Under his tutelage, I tried out occasional preaching, regularly leading worship, and developing adult education courses. I also had a chance to participate in the educational offerings he led for the congregation.

I often say that the people of Mt. Rise 'loved me into the UCC.' They supported me with so much kindness, I almost did not know how to receive it. They wanted me to succeed—I had never experienced the blessing of a community so focused on my growth and well-being. It truly was a gift of great beneficence.

Tom and Katherine came with me some of the time, but during our first year in Rochester, we had attended a local Presbyterian church where we appreciated the worship and the people. They had welcomed us and welcomed Katherine. We decided together that most of the time, Tom and Katherine would continue to attend the Presbyterian church and only come occasionally to Mt. Rise. That gave me a chance to practice being a pastor on my own and without family responsibilities on Sunday mornings.

Whether that was the right decision or not, I'm not sure. As pastors, our families participate in our ministries, and we have to learn how to balance all the responsibilities we carry. But Katherine presented a bigger challenge: in some ways, her disability made us some of the neediest members of any church we might attend. So we took the course of least resistance at the time, and attended church separately.

Learning to be a pastor is only partly about doing things—it's also about assuming a particular role within a community. At Mt. Rise, there was a large family that had many foster children. On a Sunday morning that they brought a new child to church, I watched as one of the children that had been with them for a long time pointed first to Karl, and then to me. 'That's one,' said the child. 'And that's the other one.'

Orientation was in progress and I was now included in the ranks of the pastors of the church!

Sunday mornings were the highlights of my week. I was received with respect and love at Mt. Rise, and I was successful in whatever I led. Then I would go home, dreading the work and heaviness that I knew I would feel as I walked in the door. So I'd leave home eagerly and early to go to church, and drive home as slowly as I could. Tom and Katherine would be waiting, since their church was closer, and they rarely stayed very long after the service was over.

Several years later, I met a woman who was a member of the Presbyterian church where Katherine and Tom had worshipped. I was happy to see her, and greeted her warmly. However, I was stunned by what she said to me.

'You left your daughter with us,' she said, 'and we didn't know what to do with her. Never, never, never do that again.'

I was totally unprepared for that onslaught. Now this was several years after the time that Tom and Katherine had attended worship in that congregation, and there was not a thing I could do to ease her displeasure. At the time, I had thought things were going well, that Tom was able to worship and that Katherine was welcome in the church nursery. Apparently, she was not welcomed by everyone.

At the beginning of the school year, I attended a retreat for women clergy. Away from home for a few days, I had time to myself. I was exploring meditation and contemplative prayer and took some time to engage in these faith practices. My meditations often turned to Katherine: my deep longing for her healing would surface and I would ask God again and again to let her be normal. One morning, at this retreat, I realized that I needed healing, too. My own brokenness—my fits of anger, fears, greed, and doubt—all needed healing just as much as Katherine did.

About this time, Karl led a course on Morton Kelsey's *Dreams and the Spiritual Life* for members of Mt. Rise, and as the seminarian on staff, I attended as well. Part of the discussion was on the importance of dreams in the Bible. We studied the myriad of times that scripture says, 'God came to him/her in a dream.' So why were we ignoring these messages now?

I began to record my dreams, and in the small groups of this course, talk about what they might mean. When I was dreaming, I spent a lot of time in attics (spiritual space) and basements (the unconscious). My dreams also had me struggling through small, tight spaces and then emerging into wide open spaces. I was encouraged by my dreams to understand that God was indeed working in my life. On the one hand, I was challenged by many difficult experiences; on the other, I felt myself drawn to a larger vision of life.

Back at the seminary, I continued to be energized by the conversations around the refectory table. I remember one conversation where we explored what it means to be a human being. We were reviewing a class conversation on the theology of humanity. I tried to apply some of the scientific markers for *Homo sapiens* to Katherine. She is a human being. But she does not walk upright and her hands have too much spasticity for her thumbs to be opposable. She understands much language; how much I will never know. And rational thought: well, that depends. An intellectual handicap surely limits what her mind is capable of, yet there is a certain logic in how she operates in the world.

What is it that makes Katherine, profoundly physically and mentally disabled, a human being? She is a child of human parents. Was it the spark that flashes in her eyes? Was it her capacity to give and receive love—a capacity I have never doubted. Or was it her prayer. Tom and I always prayed with her, even as a very small child. As she got older, we would assure her that although the people around her might not understand what was on her heart, she could pray and God would hear and listen. Did she understand these things?

What I studied always brought me back to the dilemma of Katherine. Theology of God: how could an all-powerful God allow Katherine's disabilities? Was God both omnipotent and compassionate? Biblical studies: I would be drawn to the texts that described Jesus' healings. Pastoral care: how does one listen to one who does not speak?

Seminary life included regular chapel services and each student was expected to participate occasionally in their leadership. I was on the schedule in October. Professor Beverly Gaventa was preaching, and I was one of the lectors. I sat in the front of the sanctuary, just behind the pulpit, as she delivered one of her powerful sermons. She was talking about the way God's love reaches wide to include all of us—that God's love does not depend on our earning it. She mentioned persons with disabilities as persons who are valued and cherished by God. My eyes welled up with tears, but I sat stoically through the conclusion of the service. When it was over, I stood up and looked at Beverly. I could not stop myself. I began to weep.

'Your grief must come up like a wave,' she said quietly, as she invited me to lunch. Beverly reinforced the message of her sermon with her own kindness to me.

The seminary was loaded with people who cared about Katherine and who were willing to stretch themselves to meet her. She was particularly fond of Dr. Werner Lemke, one of my Old Testament professors. He would hold her on his lap and was always able to engage her and make her laugh. She liked coming to school with me because as we walked the halls or rested in the refectory my friends and professors would greet her.

There was one member of the faculty, however, who was decidedly awkward in his approach to her. He knew he should befriend the little disabled girl—after all, this was a seminary where among other things, we learned about God's inclusive love. But he just couldn't get past his rigid hellos. And Katherine, ever the litmus test for phonies, would respond to him with a little "disabled" kid stare, thereby reinforcing all his stereotypes!

One day, toward the end of the first semester, when whining and complaining were at their most fervent at the seminary, I left the seminary to head over to United Cerebral Palsy for a meeting with Katherine's teachers. While the mood at my school had been ferocious in complaint and misery, at UCP the mood was joyful and radiant. The contrast was stark. Who could account for it?

To study at a seminary is a privilege. As students and faculty, we lived with the luxury of daily study, time to reflect, think, ponder. We enjoyed good minds and mostly able bodies. Sure, we had the pressure of deadlines, papers to write and frequent evaluations. But at the preschool, the losses were extreme: bodies that didn't work properly and minds crimped by disability. Yet, on that day, one venue was joyful and engaged and loving. The other was sour and defensive. It was not the circumstances of one's life that accounted for attitude and outlook. If one could find deep wells of joy among the most damaged of children, something deeper was at work.

While we had no major upsets for Katherine during that year, what we did continue to have was daily care and frequent appointments. We met regularly with her pediatrician, her neurologist, her orthopedist, and her school. At least twice a year, the orthopedist would order new AFOs or 'ankle–foot orthotics.' These were plastic inserts that held her foot and ankle in a ninety-degree angle, stretching out the tendons and muscles in her ankle and positioning her feet. After the appointment with the orthopedist, we had to take her to the company that made the orthotics—and don't, as we did initially, forget to make an appointment or you'll have to go home and come again another day. After the orthotic had been shaped, we'd go pick it up, Katherine in tow, to make sure that it fit. Then it was time for a trip to the shoe store to find a shoe that this new plastic apparatus could fit in—usually a shoe two sizes bigger than she would otherwise wear. After that, a trip back to the orthopedist to make sure that the doctor was happy with the fit.

The numerous medical appointments were only part of what was challenging. Simple, everyday things took time. Like getting out the door. If we needed to go to the store, we couldn't just say, 'Katherine, get your jacket,' and expect her to appear at the door, ready to go. No, we had to pick her up, put on the jacket, carry her to the car, install her in her car seat, and load her stroller. When a child is an infant or very small, these are ordinary activities. But Katherine was approaching four years old, and these things were no longer ordinary. If I was alone with Katherine and needed a loaf of bread or a single item from the hardware store, I would wonder if it was worth it to go right away, with Katherine, or wait until Tom was home and one of us could run the errand alone.

Eating was another challenge. If Katherine's food was cut up, and she was seated close to the table, she could pick up pieces of food and place them in her mouth. But we couldn't use a plate for her, or that would land on the floor. So eating at our house wasn't very attractive, and I longed to be able to eat a meal for myself, without feeding another person at the same time.

During the second semester, I took a marriage and family course. One of the readings suggested that for a child to thrive, they need the parent to feel like 'my life is better because you are in it.' I struggled with guilt over that one. How could I say that my life was better because of Katherine? Oh, I loved her. I loved her fiercely. But my life seemed so much harder than everybody else's. No one else in my classes had to change diapers on their four-year-old before heading out for class. No one else came home from church meetings to care for a child who had to be literally clothed and fed. How could I say that my life was better because she was in it?

Sometimes I even wished that she could die a peaceful and early death. Everybody could feel sorry for us for a while, bring over casseroles. We could grieve and then go on with our lives—without the constant lifting, feeding, diapering, and going to doctor's appointments.

What kind of person was I? What kind of pastor could I hope to be? The dilemma was that with Katherine, I would always have to work much harder than my colleagues just to stay afloat. But if I wished for my own child to die, what was wrong with my soul?

Resentment was a constant within me and between Tom and me. We both felt our lot in life was just too hard. We felt angry at the agency that had placed Katherine with us. We loved her, but our lives had been shattered by that love. We felt aggrieved by Katherine's birth parents. Initially, we had received her as the greatest gift of our lives; now we often felt like they got off easy—living lives that didn't involve total care for another human being.

Tom was now working with a local insurance company, and bringing in some income. But we were still just getting by financially. In addition, he had outstanding debts from his Ann Arbor business and his creditors were working their way through the legal system, a scary scenario.

Tom sought legal help to help him deal with the ongoing crisis of the loss of his business. His lawyer told him that the best course of action would be bankruptcy. But neither he, nor I, felt comfortable with that direction. My concern was two-fold. Plainly, I feared for the well-being of our family. And in addition,

I was preparing to become a pastor. Would these financial foibles be my undoing? Who would want to call a pastor who had financial problems? Once again, my old friend, shame, crawled into my heart. I felt ashamed by Tom's debts—as did he—and we wanted a way out of this mess that would leave us with some modicum of integrity. We held on by our fingertips, and kept going.

Katherine was in the center of this tornado that swirled around her. As much as we could, we hid our pain from her. But that turns out to be impossible to do when a child is so totally dependent upon her caregivers. She saw the friction and bitterness that seeped into the cracks of our marriage. One day, when we were verbally cross with each other, Katherine intervened.

'Unnh, unnh, unnh,' she said.

Okay, she had our attention. First, she turned to Tom and sent out a flurry of insistent sounds. Then she turned her attention to me, with the same level of intensity.

'Oh, Katherine,' I said, 'you want Mommy and Daddy to get along with each other.'

'Ya-eh,' said the little marriage counselor on the couch.

We were both deeply touched by her intervention. In the moment, we were able to calm ourselves and return to respectful conversation. We were still in marriage counseling, and would be for some time. What Katherine did was to remind us how much it mattered to her that we get along with each other.

That spring, Mt. Rise invited Elisabeth Jud, one of the leaders of Shalom Mountain Retreat and Study Center, to lead a one-day workshop on loving-kindness. Karl Johnson paid for Tom and me to attend. Tom's mother was in town at the time, and she was willing to watch Katherine for the whole-day workshop.

Using scriptures, prayer and several breathing techniques, Jud demonstrated methods to calm the spirit and remain in communion with one another. She used a guided meditation from *A Gradual Awakening*, by Stephen Levine. 'Reflect on the painfulness, the separation, which is anger, which is envy, which is jealousy.

'Experience the tightness, the loneliness, the separateness of anger, the fire. Buddha likened anger to picking up a burning ember in your bare hands with the intention of throwing it at another, all the while being seared, burned by that anger.

'Now reflect on its opposite, on the qualities of warmth and patience which allow us space in which to exist, to flower. How the anger falls away, how the knots become untied, dissolved in that openness of warmth and patience.'

This would be a task for my lifetime: to replace my anger with open-heartedness. 'Anyone who nurses anger . . . must be brought to judgement,' said Jesus (Matthew 5:22 NEB). 'Be angry, but sin not,' wrote the author of the letter to the Ephesians (4:26). First, I would have to actually feel that anger, know it. Using this meditation as a guide, I experimented every morning. Using my breath, I would clench my heart against pain and feel the rage that separated me from others, and then breathe in the spaciousness that was loving intention. I was astonished to feel my own conscious decision-making in what I felt and how I approached my life. What I was learning was that many of our difficulties would not be 'solved' by external solutions. Externally, things might not ever be resolved. Certainly, as much as I wanted Katherine's cerebral palsy to literally go away, that was not likely to happen. And though we would eventually live with enough money and begin to restore our financial health, Tom and I would not begin to heal our relationship by outer circumstances, but by choosing respect from the inside out.

By the end of the year, things at school were moving rapidly. I had my Middler Conference, a meeting of my field education supervisor and several faculty members. I had to prepare written statements about my own progress and theology, and my advisors brought their own recommendations and evaluations.

The Middler Conference was an important event, because it determined whether or not the seminary would let you go forward to graduation. It was a big step: you didn't want to slip up, and passing it meant you had accomplished what was expected up to that point.

Mine went well; I answered challenging questions honestly and with clarity. I started my paper with the words, 'The inner life is at the heart of what it means to be a Christian,' and had to rephrase what I was saying. Yes, I believed that the life of Jesus was the center of Christian life. What was different and important for me was that I was apprehending the treasures of faith in ways that were new to me. After years of intellectual assent to the gospel, now the words of scripture were dripping deep into my soul.

After a fruitful conversation with my advisors, I was approved to continue on toward graduation. I was relieved to have made it two-thirds of the way through my coursework.

I decided that I would take Hebrew after the spring semester. It was a five-week course of living, breathing, eating, and sleeping Hebrew. It was a small class: three of us met each morning under the kindly tutelage of Dr. Lemke. It was also very hard work. After our morning class, we went home to parse verbs and memorize vocabulary. At night, I dreamed of Hebrew vocabulary!

At the end of the course, having worked so diligently on something I found difficult, I was basking in the satisfaction of my academic work. I had even done well in my Hebrew class! One evening, Tom and I took Katherine for a walk around our neighborhood. We loaded her up in the little red wagon we had modified for her, and just enjoyed the beautiful, warm evening. I remember thinking to myself, 'This is the meaning of life. To be on a walk with a child.' I was filled with a sense of well-being. My hard work was satisfying, but the great joy that filled me at that moment was simply enjoying the love of my small family.

Chapter Twelve

Listening for Grace

Over the summer, we took advantage of free time and sunny days to enjoy the beautiful surroundings of the Finger Lakes. Tom would hoist Katherine on his back, and off we'd go to hike Letchworth or Stony Brook State Parks. On Sunday afternoons, we'd get in the car and drive south, circling around Honeoye Lake and Conesus and taking in the natural beauty.

We also made our annual trek to the Midwest—a few days in Chicago with my parents and then a few days in Grand Rapids with Tom's. Katherine enjoyed seeing her grandparents. She called my mother 'Gih-de-guh' (Grandma Wierenga) and both grandpas U-buh. All of her grandparents welcomed her warmly, and she, in turn was affectionate and adoring.

We had a good time on our visits, although I was aware how much my parents had changed their tune in the years between raising us and welcoming their grandchildren. At supper one evening, Katherine began deliberating tossing food over the side of her chair. I asked her to stop. She did it again, this time looking away and dropping her load in pseudo-innocence, poor little girl who can't control her fingers. I wasn't buying it. I picked up her chair, moved it a little ways away from the table and turned her around.

'Katherine,' I said firmly. 'No food on the floor. You can come back to the table when you are ready to eat nicely.'

And my father, to my great astonishment, defended her. 'Oh, don't be so hard on her,' he said. Was this the same man who held my own feet to the fire when I was a child? What had happened to him when he became a grandpa?

I held my ground for all of twenty-one seconds, and then brought her back to the table. It was long enough. The food went in her mouth, and not on the floor, at least not with cunning abandon.

While we were in Chicago, my mother wanted us to visit her Aunt Lou, who had been so generous to us when Katherine was first diagnosed. Aunt Lou lived with Alida, a tough old woman by anyone's standards. Even in her eighties she had a crusty exterior that revealed the hardness she had to develop in her many years as a police detective. When Alida was young, she would jokingly brandish her gun before her terrified nieces and nephews. I know how frightened they were, because my mother was one of them, and even as an adult, she became a little uneasy in Alida's presence.

Katherine, however, had no fear of Alida. In fact, when Katherine was around, *Alida* was different. Alida doesn't like family gatherings. So she doesn't attend. And when family came to visit, she often spent the whole visit in her room while Aunt Lou entertained the guests. But when we brought Katherine to visit, Alida was waiting to greet us — standing outside the house — on the sidewalk.

Alida knew what it was to be an outsider. She had been one most of her life. And Alida understood the fear of being excluded from life and the pain of not being loved.

Alida looked at me and said in her thick voice, 'Takes a lot of patience to raise that child.'

And then Alida looked at Katherine. Her eyes softened and the blue in Alida's eyes was suddenly as soft and clear and young as the blue in Katherine's.

This was the mystery of Katherine. She drew some people right into her orbit and called out of them a deep well of compassion. And it was not always clear when or where it would happen. My mother eagerly introduced Katherine to one of her favorite cousins; he was not interested. But Alida, who had endured a very hard life, and faced deep personal rejection, received Katherine's magic with an open heart.

All too soon, the summer ended, and it was time for school to start again. For me, it would be the last year in the cocoon of the seminary. For Katherine, it was a continuation of her program at United Cerebral Palsy.

Katherine's seat on her bus was in the very last row. It was a small bus, it comprised only six rows of two seats each, and it was not full. By the time she got on, identical twins, Matthew and Edward, were also aboard and they had worked out a daily routine for me to follow. On the way to the back of the bus, Edward would stick his legs out into the aisle, and I would have to ask him to let me through. On the way back to the front, it would be Matthew's turn to block my passage and it was Matthew who I would have to ask to let me through. Or was it Matthew and then Edward? This was accompanied by a lot of giggling and smirking. I couldn't help but smile myself as I carried Katherine to her seat, buckled her in, and then made my way back off the bus.

Rascals to the core, the twins spoke little, but were physically quite capable. One day, Matthew threw his glasses out the window and when his mother asked where they were, he laughed and pointed out the window. Another day, a new bus driver sailed past our house with Katherine in the back seat. It was a small child, with a series of sounds and gestures, who guided the driver back up the street to our front door.

My classes were rigorous: I was taking a New Testament course on the epistles of Paul, a preaching course , as well as classes in history and worship. For the New Testament class, I had to write a lengthy study of Romans 6:12–14:

Therefore, do not let sin exercise dominion in your mortal bodies, to make you obey their passions. No longer present your members to sin as instruments of wickedness, but present yourselves to God as those who have been brought from death to life, and present your members to God as instruments of righteousness. For sin will have no dominion over you since you are not under law, but under grace.

Having spent so much time analyzing the text, it was a natural fit as the text for my first sermon in preaching class. I felt pretty confident about the project, and made my required appointment with my preaching professor to discuss my sermon. *A half-hour in his office*, I thought to myself, *and this will come together nicely.*

I met with him. After our conversation, I discovered I had not one direction to pursue, but several. I became a little more anxious about the prospect of turning my ideas into a sermon, but still eager.

And then I left the seminary to keep another appointment. This one was at Katherine's school. The physical therapist had determined that it was time for Katherine to move from an ordinary stroller to a wheelchair!

Purchasing a wheelchair is no small task. Because of the complexity of Katherine's disabilities, she needed something called a 'positioning chair' built to her exact needs. Katherine and I met with the physical therapist and a representative from the wheelchair company. Katherine was carefully measured and the PT gave specifics about what she felt would hold Katherine in correct sitting posture. This would enable Katherine to use her arms more effectively (because she would be seated upright) and to keep her legs and hips in alignment.

But specifications aside, to purchase that wheelchair meant I had to swallow another big lump of pain. Sure, the wheelchair made life easier for Katherine and for us. But at the time we bought it, all I could think was, *My little girl is disabled. Oh, no! Oh, God, no!*

Meanwhile I was attempting to craft a sermon on Romans 6. Suddenly the words of the text began to catch in my throat. Do—not—let—sin—rule—in your mortal bodies.

Katherine's body does not grow straight and cannot move. Do

not let sin rule? What choice does she have? She bears the marks of human brokenness in her own body, and no sin of hers put them there.

Frustrated and angry, I tried to work on the sermon without thinking about Katherine, but something in the text itself demanded my attention. I tensed up, worried about meeting the deadline looming over me.

The best advice I've ever heard for preachers who get stuck is to return to the text. So back to the text I went, struggling to find the meaning in the words.

'Yield,' place, locate, present! Present as an offering or sacrifice. And the light went on. 'To present as an offering or sacrifice.' Under the law, no priest could be disabled. The lamb must be unblemished. Cain had rendered his first-fruits and never understood why his sacrifice was rejected.

What a burden it is to need to make a perfect sacrifice, to be whole before coming to God!

Who could come before the Lord?

Surely not Katherine—and surely not me!

The sermon was pressing against me, pushing me to under-stand what it might mean for Katherine—and for me—to live, not according to law, but under grace. I wrote:

Law says, 'You must be whole to enter.'
Grace says, 'Enter; you will be made whole.'

Law says, 'You can't see where you are going.'
Grace says, 'I am here beside you.'

Law says, 'You are not strong enough to walk.'
Grace says, 'I will carry you.'

Law says, 'Don't get your hopes up.'
Grace says, 'Your future is open.'

I had a sermon. Or, perhaps, I should say, the sermon had me. I was grasped by something, someone who held me, and would not let me go.

The semester moved by quickly. Soon exams were over and we were preparing for Christmas. When we asked Katherine what she wanted for Christmas, she responded, 'Bwuh, Bwuh.' We asked several times and got the same response, so we knew that she had something definite in mind. How distressing it was for us to know she had something on her mind that we could not understand! Perhaps it was a blessing in disguise that it took us until March to figure it out, however.

Katherine wanted a dog—a bow-wow!

I'm still not sure how we ever figured that one out, but we did, and when we asked Katherine about it, she verified our hunch with her very confident and definite 'Ya-eh.' In hindsight, it made sense. Her friend, April, had had a birthday in November, and her present was a dog. And Katherine loved dogs, cats and other animals. So it seemed entirely reasonable to Katherine. But it seemed so unreasonable to us; we had no clue what was going on in her head. Christmas came, and Christmas went, but that Christmas we couldn't give Katherine her heart's desire. When we did finally figure it out, we reluctantly told her that a dog was not in the offing for our family.

In January, between semesters, we had another challenge. Katherine was going to go back to Newington Hospital for yet another hip surgery. I responded to this crisis numbly, frustrated that in my first semester of seminary—and now my last— Katherine would have to have a serious surgery. This time, I drove with Katherine alone, and Tom would come later in the week to drive us home. The front wheels of the new wheelchair collapsed into the body of the chair, making it function as a super-sturdy car seat. Katherine was a good traveler, but even so, the six-hour drive was a challenge.

We got a later start than we planned, and then, just as we hit the Mass Pike, we had a blow-out. At first, I didn't know what it was. All I knew was that suddenly my little red Horizon was swerving down the highway, and I had to grip the wheel tightly to get the car back into control and off to the side of the road.

It was as I'd feared. The rear passenger-side tire was completely ripped apart. As I stood beside the car in the early dusk, preparing to change the tire — and breathing deeply in fear on this busy road — a large semi pulled up and stopped behind me. I didn't know whether to be frightened or grateful. But the driver was kind and offered to change the tire for me, while I waited in the warm car with Katherine. As he finished, he told me the best place in Springfield, Massachusetts, to purchase a new tire and then said, 'I thought I'd see who got out of the car. If it was a man, I'd just drive by. But since you were a woman, I decided to stop and help.'

For all my carefully honed feminism, at that moment, I was just grateful for the rescue.

Because we were now even later, we bypassed a stop for supper to head straight to the hospital. I knew they would have food at the hospital, and I didn't want to delay our arrival anymore. What I was not prepared for was that moments after leading us to Katherine's room, they came for her blood work.

'This child hasn't eaten,' I said. 'Could you please wait?'

They couldn't. Katherine was completely miserable. She was hungry, tired, and back in a place that she knew would hurt her. Taking her blood at that moment was adding insult to injury.

After she was settled, I had to go back downstairs to the admitting office to fill out forms and sign papers. We had been studying Abraham and Isaac. I personally have a very difficult time with the story in which Abraham is prepared to sacrifice his only son. At this moment, I felt like Abraham. My own hand would not lift the knife — I had only to lift a pen and give permission for someone else to cut her open. Still, just when I would think that I was coming to terms with the difficulties presented by Katherine's disability, along would come another challenge, another hurdle, and another stomach-turning experience.

Once again, Katherine endured the surgery, and came through like a trooper. But her sleep time was being interrupted with regularly grating frequency. By the second day, she had barely gotten any sleep and was uncomfortable and unhappy. Finally, singing and humming and standing near her, I helped her get to sleep. Then I went and stood in the doorway of her room.

A few minutes later, one of the hospital vampires arrived at the door with the little basket of equipment for drawing blood. I glared at him. He looked at my face, then took a quick step back and said, 'I guess this isn't a good time for me to come in.'

I growled at him. 'I guess not.' I remained at my post until Katherine woke up naturally, and began to feel a little bit better.

Each time that Katherine was casted, the exact shape of the cast was determined by the best positioning of her hip. She would be X-rayed while still in surgery, and then Dr. Gage and his team would place her legs and hips in the best position for healing. This time, her cast came out almost as if she was seated. And now that she had her fancy positioning wheelchair, it was possible to rig it up so that she could use it during her recovery.

We went down to the on-site orthotics shop at the hospital, and a saint in that workroom crafted a new wide foot rest, made a few adjustments and sent Katherine home able to use her wheelchair as usual. This turned out to be a very lucky break. Her care during the casting procedure would still be more challenging than usual, but because of this arrangement, most of our regular activities could go on as planned.

When I took Katherine to the seminary, she really wanted to spend some time on Dr. Lemke's lap once again. He wasn't sure how this would work, but he was brave. Carefully, I helped balance her on his knee, and she was delighted to be back in business once again.

This cast was going to come off in Rochester. There were some pins in her hip from the surgery that would be removed as well, so this required a short stay in Genesee Hospital for these relatively minor procedures. When my mother came to help out, Katherine poured out her heart in a stream of syllables and sound. We didn't know exactly what she was saying, but she was unhappy—especially with me for bringing her to the hospital—and grateful to have a loving grandma to share her sorrow.

The next night, I was alone in the hospital with her. My brother, Ed, showed up, carrying a little brown paper bag. He opened it, and lifted out a Barbie thermos. 'Do you have any cups?' he asked.

I ran down the hall to the little kitchen on the floor and snagged a couple of hospital-issue plastic glasses. He opened the thermos and filled our cups with vodka gimlets. Then he reached into his shirt pocket, pulled out a zip-top sandwich baggie and pulled out two slices of lime. As we sat beside Katherine's bedside, I thought it was one of the kindest things anyone had done for me. Such was our mirth that even Katherine seemed a little cheerier because of my improved mood.

By now, I was coming to the end of the second semester, final papers and exams, and graduation. I had lost a little time preparing my profiles and resumé—it was all I could do to finish my coursework and care for Katherine. Looking for work would have to wait until after graduation.

One day, I found a green sheet of paper in my seminary mail box. Torn at the bottom, it was a request from the Director of the Library, Peter Vanden Berg, to stop by to see him as soon as I could. Peter kept his desk in the lobby of the library. How he ever got any work done in that milieu, I could not understand, but he did. Every night, he cleared off his desk completely, and every morning, set himself up again. He was always accessible to the students and faculty of the school and a genuinely kind presence.

I went to see him. He talked slowly, reminding me of my Dutch father-in-law. 'You know,' he said, 'we have a Trost prize, for the student who is most likely to be an effective preacher, pastor and parish minister.'

I did. It was a coveted prize, not only for the recognition, but also because the award came with a stipend for purchasing books.

'And this year,' he drawled on, 'that person is you.'

I was astonished and thrilled. Peter's taciturn announcement was in direct contrast to my excitement. I tried to keep my enthusiasm in check as I floated back to my classes and home for the day. I told Tom, but otherwise I kept the secret until graduation, when the award was formally announced.

Graduation. It had been an almost unbelievable three years. But here I was, wearing cap and gown, and entertaining all our family for the weekend. Both sets of parents came for commencement on Saturday, and to hear me preach at Mountain Rise on Sunday. When I was called up to receive the Trost Award, Tom stood up and gave me a standing ovation. We had made it. Not only was I graduating, I had received a prestigious award.

But where were the awards for patience in raising my disabled daughter, or for excellence in changing diapers? The hardest part of my life was hidden away, and would be recognized only in passing.

Chapter Thirteen

Wise Child

Now at last it was time for me to search for a job in earnest. The bill collectors had tapered off a little—in part, because some of Tom's creditors had moved to taking judgments against him, and weren't bothering with harassment anymore. We knew that if I had a job, and we sold our home, we'd be able to pay off the debts and live with a bit more sanity.

At this point in the story, we were open to moving anywhere, although my first interview was for a church in Henrietta, a suburb of Rochester, just six-and-a-half miles from where we were living. The search committee of Henrietta United Church of Christ was preparing to offer me the position—and they let me know that—but a series of small difficulties in the congregation meant that they would have to delay making the final offer.

It was a time of intense anxiety for me. I knew I needed to work, and was attracted to this local congregation. In addition, it was the home congregation of Antoinette Brown Blackwell, the first woman ordained in the United States. The year I was being called was the 150th anniversary of her ordination, and the congregation was actively celebrating her life and ministry. It was daunting, of course, and humbling, but the thought of following in her footsteps was a privilege that gave me courage.

One of the congregation's strengths was a ministry they had in place with adults with handicapping conditions who lived in a nearby group home. They were interested in my candidacy at least partly because they knew I would be someone who was willing and interested in encouraging them in this ministry.

As much as I was willing and eager to work, I was also terrified. Would I be able to meet all the demands of parish ministry? Would I be up to the task? Would anyone really want me as their pastor? I continued to search and was invited to interview at two churches in different cities in Wisconsin.

I put together elaborate travel plans that had me fly into Grand Rapids, Michigan, with Katherine. We would stay for a day with Tom's parents and meet up with my family at a family reunion in Michigan. Then my parents would drive us to Chicago. They'd take care of Katherine while I drove one of their cars to the interviews.

My parents were just a little uneasy taking care of Katherine without me. Since there was one day between my two interviews, I told them that I could easily come back to Chicago between the two interviews. I also left them my trademark copious pages of information about Katherine's schedule, likes, dislikes and a lexicon to her small vocabulary. Feeling a bit nervous myself, I left for my interviews.

The morning after I finished the first interview, I called home to see how they were doing.

No answer.

I drove a little farther down the road and called again.

No answer.

Finally, it was getting late and I had to make a decision. Should I find a hotel and stay up in Wisconsin, or should I just head back to Chicago to see how things were going? I made one last phone call.

They were home. Well, no, why would they be at home—? They'd taken Katherine to Lincoln Park Zoo where they all had had a lovely day. Well, no, why did I think I should return to Chicago? There were no problems and Katherine was just so much fun to have around. 'She's the big cheese,' my mother reported. 'I say to her, "Are you the big cheese?" and she laughs and laughs.'

Apparently, I was not needed. In my absence my parents lost their fear of caring for Katherine and forged a deeper bond with her.

Meanwhile, I heard from the first church I had visited in Wisconsin. They were prepared to offer me a position as their associate pastor. I was glad that the interview went well, but I was conflicted. How would it work to move to Wisconsin? We'd be closer to both sets of parents and that would be a good thing. Tom was planning to start a new company, and he could live almost anywhere to do it. Wisconsin had an active contingent of churches in my denomination and strong conference leadership. But we would have to check out schools and physicians for Katherine. That in itself made a move there seem daunting.

That night, after I had settled into my hotel, a note was slipped under my door. 'Call home,' it said.

I called Tom back in Rochester and was thrilled to learn that the Henrietta United Church of Christ was ready to call me as their pastor. My palpable relief told me this was the right place not only for me, but for my family. Adjusting to life in ministry would be tough enough; resettling Katherine in Wisconsin may have been beyond my strength.

Now life swung into high gear. I accepted the offer from the Henrietta United Church of Christ and met with the church search committee. We hammered out a contract.

The Henrietta United Church of Christ was a congregation that had been in Henrietta since the early part of the nineteenth century. Twenty years before my arrival, they had replaced the old white clapboard structure with a sixties modern building and new parsonage. When I was pastor, we had about 120 people in worship on a Sunday morning. It was an active congregation with lots of lay leaders, a passion for outreach ministries, a strong education program, and an informal style of operating. It was reshaping itself from a rural church serving a farming community to the suburban church it was becoming.

The next step in the United Church of Christ call system is to preach what is called a 'Candidating Sermon.' After the service is finished, the candidate is whisked away from the church, while the congregation votes for their new pastor. Bill and Jane Stratton were elected to take Tom, Katherine and me out for lunch while the congregation deliberated. Jane and Bill had three children; their middle child, Ellen, also had serious disabilities and their youngest, Eric, was a small dynamo. We went to Cartwright's Inn for a Sunday brunch. The restaurant wisely situated our party in a small back room. Just as we were getting seated, the chair of the search committee and the moderator of the council roared up with the news. Only one negative vote! I was in!

Having called their new pastor, the search committee made arrangements for our move. We began cleaning out our house and put it on the market.

Moving is never a chore I enjoy, but this move came with a big piece of relief. We loaded up boxes of books and dishes. As I disassembled my little study, I pulled down the 'Do not pray for an easy life; pray to be a strong person' poster that had encouraged me throughout seminary. But now, despite the fact that I was entering the ministry, I pulled it down and left it in the trash. I knew I would need strength for my new life, but I was also conscious of the huge demands in my life, and resentful that nothing seemed to come easy for me. I did not want to think my life would always be so difficult.

Moving to a parsonage meant that our house could be sold. We still had very little money, but we did have some equity in our home, and were looking forward to being released from our debt. We could pay off the remaining debt, and still have a little cash left over. Not much, but something. When we met with our lawyer, as he filed all the papers, he read aloud the releases from judgment. For each of five judgments that had been taken, he said, 'This has been paid in full and the judgment is released.'

It sounded a lot like the theology of St. Paul to me, but what relief flooded over me as I heard those words! Tom had one creditor who had not taken a judgment against him, and instead accepted work in payment when Tom started his new business later that fall. The onerous burden of debt had been lifted.

The whole fall moved along in a frantic, hectic blur. The only day we could engage the moving van was two weeks after I started in Henrietta! On the day of our move, a big truck pulled into our driveway early in the morning. 'Kuk,' said Katherine. 'Kuk.'

We had arranged for a friend from Mountain Rise, Linda, to pick her up from school that day. As a special treat, Katherine was going to stay overnight at Linda's house with Linda and her niece, Christa. Linda drove a Trans Am which Katherine thought was very cool. She referred to it as 'in-dis-gah' (Linda's car).

The parsonage was a large four-bedroom home, just off the parking lot from the church. Tom helped with some of the painting to get the house ready. We put up some wallpaper in Katherine's new room, and instead of her crib, installed a junior-sized bed that had come from Tom's family. Katherine loved her 'big girl bed.' However, it didn't take long for her to figure out how to wriggle out of it and land on the floor.

Two weeks after we moved, the trustees of the church replaced the kitchen cabinets in the parsonage and two weeks after that I was ordained. I came to associate the ministry with terminal exhaustion!

One of the blessings of my new congregation was how fully they welcomed and included Katherine. Because of the ministry they already had going with adults with disabilities, they were already comfortable with persons who have handicapping condi-tions. When we had been there just a few weeks, there was a Halloween party for the children of the church. Katherine was invited — and I wasn't. This was amazing to me — to bring her to a church function and let her participate without my hovering presence.

At Christmas time, the Church School teachers planned their annual pageant. My job was to read the Christmas story from Luke 2, while the children marched into the sanctuary: a little

Mary and Joseph, toting a baby doll; accompanied by assorted shepherds, wise boys and girls, donkeys and angels. I looked up as I got to the part where suddenly the multitude of the heavenly host appears, and there was Katherine adorned with white robe and a halo of silver tinsel! Judy Green and Cindy Richards had dressed her in a white angel costume complete with the halo. I nearly choked on the lump that ballooned in my throat. With tears now seeping from my eyes, I continued, 'Glory to God in the highest, and on earth, peace.'

Later, I asked Judy how they managed to get the halo on my little angel's head. After all, Katherine never liked anything on her head, and managed to pull off any hat we might ever attempt to put there. Judy explained that while Cindy distracted Katherine, she had crept behind our girl and slipped the tinsel on her head. Katherine was none the wiser, and had just starred in her first Christmas pageant.

Tom left the insurance company and began a new business, The Scholar's Choice, through which he exhibited academic books at conferences of scholars. That meant he would have to travel. When he was at home, he worked out of the basement of the parsonage. He would be close at hand during the day and could retrieve Katherine from the bus in the afternoons when I was working. The challenge was covering the evenings when Tom was away and I had meetings.

Enter the young teenagers from the church who became her babysitters. Sisters Lisa and Mary Karen Eckardt and their friend, Julie Kilbourne, took turns helping us with Katherine. They also become her friends. It was refreshing and delightful to see them interact with Katherine in such loving, playful ways. In turn, Katherine adored them and poured out her admiration in ways that only she could do. A side benefit was that meetings when I had youthful babysitters had to end by 9:45 pm so that the girls could get home on time.

The church building was home to a daycare program,

Community Concerns Childcare, led by Alice DeVinney. They welcomed Katherine into their program. We didn't need a lot of time at daycare; she continued to attend the United Cerebral Palsy preschool during the day, and most afternoons, Tom or I were able to meet her bus. She would go to childcare on Wednesday afternoons and during some school holidays. She liked being with the other children, and they in turn were being encouraged to greet her and include her in their play when they could. On the other afternoons, one of us often took her for a walk that would include stopping to visit the children when they played outside on the parking lot and play area.

The first days of ministry were profoundly challenging to me. I felt competent at each of the discrete tasks of my profession: a pastoral visit, preparing for worship, preaching. But putting together the whole package felt like a juggling act in which I was frequently dropping balls. What I learned in seminary gave me a basis; now I had to learn a set of skills and practices that could only be acquired on the job. Indeed, I had to make the adjustments that come with life in a parsonage. I swung between excitement at my new work and constant anxiety that I was missing something. I had to adjust to people who didn't know me well making judgments about my life. But I came to enjoy the pastoral role, and the open invitation into the lives of the people I served.

In March of that first year, I had to conduct a funeral for the first time. This was a significant loss for the congregation—the sudden death of an active, beloved church leader. The church was full, and I was anxious about how well I would be able to lead this event. But what I hadn't prepared for was Katherine's reaction. We had told her we would go to the funeral and explained what it was. She was upset and fussy that afternoon. We sat with her and tried to figure out what was bothering her.

Finally, I asked, 'Do you think if Mommy and Daddy go to the funeral, *we* will die?'

'Ya-eh.'

We were able to correct her misperception and she relaxed, confident that we would return home after the service.

As she became more aware of her world, it was challenging to figure out what was going on in her head. For example, one day we were talking with her about being a baby. We had a little book of her baby pictures which we called, 'The Story of Baby Katherine,' and we liked looking at these together. We were talking about baby Katherine, and she said clearly, 'Adaw.'

Adaw.

'You were adopted when you were a baby.'

'Ya-eh.'

Another day she came home from school frustrated. Out of her mouth came these sounds: 'Ee wah waw.'

I want to walk.

But for every time we understood what she meant, there were many times that we didn't. And sometimes she would say something once, like the sentence about wanting to walk, and then we'd never hear about it again. She was remarkably calm when she couldn't have what she asked for. She would be hugely relieved that we understood what she wanted, but then if we told her it wasn't possible, she would remain relaxed. It often seemed to us that just being understood was what mattered most to her.

About this time, she was scheduled to be evaluated by a psychologist. Now six years old, she would have to transfer to a new program in the coming fall. As part of the preparation for that move, she was referred to a developmental psychologist. I went to school to be with her during the testing.

The little rascal skewed everything! She sat through the whole interview as if she knew nothing! I was exasperated. She didn't want to put the block in the cup or touch the baby doll or give any indication at all that she understood what was going on. 'She doesn't seem to understand the concept of putting one object into another,' pronounced the doctor.

I was frustrated and angry with Katherine. I knew she understood more than she was letting on. I was also angry with the psychologist. There was a little section in the interview for the parent to add their comments. But I felt like it was a sop. I was afraid that the report would include something like 'Crazy, unrealistic, overprotective mother thinks her child is a genius.'

Of greater concern to me was that this evaluation was the basis upon which a recommendation would be made for her school placement. Mary Cariola Children's Center was being recommended. The school has a great reputation. But how could I trust the recommendations of this psychologist when the results he had to work with missed so much of what Katherine was capable of?

I knew. She did not walk. Her speech was limited to a few vocalizations. She could not feed herself or move her arms. She didn't toddle around the house or draw pictures or play ball. But she knew what 'Touch the doll' meant and how to put something in the cup. And she also knew that sometimes the only power she had was *not* to do what was expected of her.

The evaluation occurred in March. It was the season of Lent and at church we had received little cardboard boxes to make a daily contribution to help the poor. Each night at supper, as we concluded our meal, we would read from a little devotional book and put a few coins in the box. Katherine loved this daily ritual and participated with great satisfaction.

We came home from the evaluation in which the psychologist confidently told us she didn't understand the concept of putting something in. At our dinner table, I asked Katherine if she wanted to put money into the Lenten box. Katherine cheerfully grasped a quarter in the center of her twisted palm, and with jerky, shifting movements, brought her hand over the box and let go of the coin.

Even with all my frustration, I found myself laughing. She was not predictable—or maybe she was. Putting the coin in the

Lenten box had meaning for her. It was an opportunity for her to give, and it represented her participation in our church. But putting a cube in a cup was just plain boring to her, and represented evaluation and judgment. Katherine might be mentally and physically handicapped, but she was also wise beyond her disabilities.

Chapter Fourteen

Little Pockets of Mystery

The Abbey of the Genesee is a Trappist monastery located a short drive south of Henrietta. In my first years of ministry, I would occasionally drive south to the abbey for a day of contemplation and prayer. The monks were very generous with their space; you could sit quietly in one of the rooms they reserved for their guests and then join the monks for their peaceful worship.

Trappists maintain silence throughout much of their day. The idea is that extraneous talk impedes the relationship with God. So they move through their days with a rhythm of work, silence and prayer. The community they maintain is a container of peacefulness, and as I discovered in those early days in a parish, a place of welcome and respite.

There is usually one monk whose job it is to welcome guests. On one of my visits, I had a conversation with the monk who was on hospitality duty. He had lived for many years at another Trappist monastery, Gethsemane, known as the abbey that was once home to Thomas Merton. I asked him about Merton, and about life in the monastery. I will never forget what he said to me.

'Without speech, you can really get to know what a person is like.'

Without speech.

Katherine's lack of speech was one of the hardest things about her care. We could sometimes understand what she was driving at; at other times we were completely clueless. And sometimes, we had no idea at all what was important to her. I used to say, 'There are three categories: I know I know, I know I don't know, and I don't know if I know.'

It had not occurred to me that there could be a hidden awareness that emerged not in spite of, but because of, the lack of speech.

Trappists, of course, can speak. But at certain times and places, they choose not to. And not only does their silence allow an entrance for God in their lives; in quiet observation of one another, they come to know the members of their own community more deeply.

We did know Katherine well. We knew what comforted her, we knew that she really liked Coca-Cola, and we knew of her deep appreciation for Mr. Rogers. I knew that when I arrived home late at night, after a church meeting, she would wake up upon my arrival and quickly fall back to sleep after I kissed her goodnight. For all the times that Tom and I agonized over what might be on her mind, there were many times that in listening to her affect and not her words, we understood her well. And she knew us. She cooed when we were happy and offered her 'luh, luh, luh' (love, love, love) sounds when we were sad. As hard as her daily care still was for us, we discovered little pockets of mystery.

Her care continued to be difficult. She was larger now and therefore more difficult to manage. Though she was smaller than the average five-year-old, she was larger than a child who is always carried. The parsonage was a large two-story affair, so we needed not only to lift her in and out of her bed and wheelchair; we also carried her up and down the stairs.

I tried to get regular exercise at a local gym, but even when I did, it wasn't enough to prevent my back from aching. I asked my doctor once why I wasn't just building muscle from all the lifting. 'It's a repetitive strain,' he told me.

Small comfort.

When I was home alone with her, I monitored how many trips I made up and down the stairs with her. On a Saturday, for example, I might get her up in the morning and wash and dress her upstairs. Then I would carry her downstairs and install her in her wheelchair for breakfast and a morning in front of the TV.

I would keep her in her wheelchair through lunch and then I would put her on a blanket on the floor to play. This was planned to keep her moving, but to limit the number of times I lifted her in and out of her chair or bed. I planned my day so that she could be near me while I worked in my home study or in the kitchen. I experienced myself as 'tethered' to her when I was with her.

I worked hard at church. There were meetings to attend, newsletters to write, sermons to prepare, pastoral visits to make. But I was conscious always that I had to budget my time and energy. Occasionally, I would be asked to do something beyond the walls of the church—something at the conference or association levels of the church. I weighed these opportunities very carefully, trying to balance my precariously overloaded life.

In September, Katherine began going to the Mary Cariola Children's Center. Mary Cariola is a wonderful program for children with serious disabilities, named after its founder. Katherine found a warm welcome at Mary Cariola and adjusted quickly to her new routines. We knew she had found a good place when shortly after she arrived, they said of Katherine, 'She has a very independent spirit.'

They got her!

Our first social worker at Mary Cariola was a breath of fresh air named Pat Sabadhakari. Pat was understanding, efficient and knew exactly what resources were available and how to access them. She quickly discovered Katherine did not have a separate car seat and set about to order one and get it paid for. She did the same thing for a 'Pogon buggy'—a large, collapsible stroller that was easier to transport than her wheelchair, and more flexible for taking on family outings.

When I talked with Pat, she was always full of respect for Katherine and for our family. One day, describing the children of Mary Cariola, she told me, 'Our kids live in a world of relationship.'

Her words rang true. We knew Katherine to be a social, loving being.

'Our kids live in a world of relationship,' she continued, 'because that is all they have.'

Possessions mean very little to someone who cannot use or manipulate those possessions without assistance. All that matters is to be around people who are loving and dependable. We learned the phrase 'non-self-preserving,' a term used technically by caregivers to denote the ability of a person to save him or herself from a burning building. What a horrifying phrase! Katherine was not 'self-preserving.' She could not save herself but would always depend on the courage and kindness of others. Our daughter lived in a world of relationship!

Tom and I, however, still lived in the world of conflicting obligations and limited resources. One of our needs was for a larger car to accommodate Katherine. But my salary was very small, and even with the parsonage it was tough to make ends meet. Tom's business was just beginning, and he was not yet taking a salary. On one of our visits with Dr. McBride, she asked pointedly about any needs we might have.

'I'd really like to get a van,' I admitted. 'But we simply can't afford it.'

She responded by suggesting that there might be help for us. She told us it certainly couldn't hurt if we were to ask around. So we did. We asked the Adoption Subsidy program, we talked to Pat, and we sent a note to the agency where Katherine had been adopted. We didn't really expect anything to happen, but hey, you never know!

In January, I was working at my home desk when the phone rang. It was Harold Wiersma, the social worker who had helped us when we adopted Katherine. He had quietly followed our progress in the days since she had been placed, and had been concerned and saddened by her disabilities. Now he was calling me with what he said was good news.

It was. The agency occasionally had donors who would offer

to help out with a need that was unusual or couldn't be met any other way. He had found a donor that was willing to buy a van for us!

'This man adopted his children through our agency,' Harold reported. 'He is a Christian man who has been very successful in business, and wanted to share some of his riches with others.'

Tom and I were amazed and grateful. We headed out to a car dealer as soon as we had a little time and found the car we hoped to buy: a Plymouth Voyager. We wouldn't need a lift yet, just a vehicle that was large enough to accommodate Katherine, her wheelchair and the loaded tote bags we took everywhere we went. Tom went back alone to negotiate the price and finalize the deal.

'Well,' said the dealer after an hour of haggling, 'we're only a hundred dollars apart on our price.'

Tom smiled back. 'I can spend another hour with you for a hundred dollars.'

The dealer met his price and we had new wheels that had come to us in an astonishing way. We had been given enough money to buy the mini-van we needed. It wasn't the miracle I'd been praying for all these years, but it was still a miracle!

One afternoon in early spring, I was visiting with a parishioner when I happened to mention that Katherine had wanted a dog. We thought it would be a good idea, I said, but had not gotten our act together to actually look for a dog for our family.

'My neighbor's dog just had puppies,' she volunteered. 'They're very nice dogs. The family is getting ready to move, so they want to give the puppies away for free.'

It happened almost that fast. My parishioner called her neighbor and then called me. She set up a meeting for us with the family to check out the dogs. Tom and I were completely enthralled. We were able to see the parents: a black Labrador and golden retriever and they were beautiful dogs. The puppies, of course, were completely adorable. There was one little puppy who held back a little from the wriggling crowd. He was a lovely tan color. That was it. We were smitten. We hadn't really decided to add a puppy to our already full life. We just did it.

This was Thursday afternoon, and since we had obligations that would take us away from home over the weekend, we made arrangements to bring the dog home on Monday afternoon.

When Katherine came home from school, we told her the good news. She eyed us suspiciously, as if to say, 'My parents. A dog? I don't believe it.'

We collected a crate, a book on training and various assorted puppy needs. Then we spent the weekend choosing a name. We came up with 'Caleb' because it means 'dog' in Hebrew. At last I was making use of the five weeks, twelve hours a day I had spent working on the language!

Monday afternoon, we were ready when Katherine came home from school. We drove over to meet the family who had our dog and plucked him out of the pen. Our new little squirming puppy sat with Katherine and me in the back seat of our van.

How she loved this new puppy! She lay on the floor and let him crawl over her. He let her pull his ears and reach out for him. He was a most gentle dog, except if he felt Katherine might be threatened. We threw balls across the church parking lot and watched him churn his legs to run after it. We had a dog!

I'm not sure what made us think we could take on this new responsibility—other than we didn't think very much. The whole process happened so fast, we just blew past all our reservations. This is not necessarily a good thing, but this time, it worked for us.

The dog himself was free, but by the time we'd taken him to the vet and bought a few doggie necessities, we'd spent well over a hundred dollars for our free dog. What did work was that Tom's office was at home and mine was just across the parking lot. We crate-trained Caleb, and he was house-broken pretty quickly. Between the church parking lot and the greenbelt behind the church, he had plenty of room to run. When he was still very small I took him with me on some pastoral calls—he was a big hit with my elderly farmers. I also took him with me when I wanted to hike alone in a local park.

But it was for Katherine that we took the risk of a dog, and it was to Katherine that Caleb was most devoted. He went out with her to the bus in the morning and greeted her in the afternoon. He willingly cleaned up the floor as she was eating and he sat beside her chair when she watched TV. When we took Katherine for a walk, Caleb went, too. And Katherine was delighted that we had this wonderful new family member.

Katherine continued her Wednesday afternoons at the childcare. She also went there during school breaks. At the end of one week, the center had planned a trip to the zoo. Because it would be a challenge to care for Katherine on a large bus and in that environment, Alice DeVinney asked me if I could keep Katherine home that day. It was a Friday and I would be working at home, so I easily agreed.

The next morning, Katherine woke up very early. She was giggly and excited.

'You're pretty happy today, Katherine,' I said. 'What's so exciting?'

'Ooooo,' she said. 'Oooooo.'

She was planning to go to the zoo. Katherine didn't understand that when daycare staff talked about the zoo, they weren't intending to take her. I wrestled with what to do. Then I went to another room and made a clandestine phone call to Alice.

'Katherine thinks she's going to the zoo,' I told her. 'Is there any way at all to make it possible for her to go?'

I really did not want to disappoint my little girl.

Fortunately, neither did Alice. God bless her! She and I brainstormed for a few minutes—I told her I understood if we needed to stay with the original plan, but I did not want to break

Katherine's heart. Alice and I figured out that they could use her car seat on the bus and use her little red wagon to pull her through the zoo. Katherine was thrilled and so proud of herself to go on this outing with all the other children.

The other piece of this blessing is that it worked well for the group. The little red wagon that held Katherine also toted some lunches and other necessities. Katherine was so happy to be with them. Her joy was contagious and the staff felt valued and appreciated.

Life was full and rich for us. The church was flourishing. I was learning to deal with the ups and downs of parish ministry, and Tom's new little company was starting to earn actual income. Nevertheless, we were working hard. When summer came, we were eager and ready for a short trip to Old Forge, a three-hour drive into the Adirondack region of New York State.

We arrived tired and weary, ready for a break. We found a hotel room and settled in for the night. About midnight, I woke up to the sounds of sirens.

'I think there's a fire somewhere,' I said, waking Tom from a sound sleep.

'And it's here!' he shouted.

Sure enough, we saw a red light spinning right outside our door. We threw on our jeans and shirts. I wrapped Katherine in a blanket and carried her sleepy little body across the parking lot and found a bench away from the action.

Tom pulled Katherine's wheelchair out of the room and away from any possible danger. Then he moved our van to the other side of the parking lot and went door to door waking people up.

By now Katherine was wide awake and watching with wide eyes.

'Bwhuh, Bwhuh,' she announced.

'Baby Bear?' I asked. 'Are you worried about Baby Bear?' Baby Bear was a favorite stuffed animal and he had made the trip with us. 'Baby Bear is safe,' I said.

'Nnnh,' said Katherine. 'Bwhuh, Bwhuh.'

'Book, do you want your book?'

'Nnnh. Bwhuh, Bwhuh.'

This continued for some time. I was running out of b-words, so I tried Daddy, the van, her wheelchair, anything else I could think of.

She was insistent. 'Bwhuh, Bwhuh,' she said with increasing intensity.

And suddenly the light dawned.

'Do you want to pray, Katherine?' I said. 'Is that it?'

There was one word Katherine could say, and she could use an inflection that let me understand in no uncertain terms that she couldn't figure out what took me so long.

'Ya-eh.'

So we prayed. We prayed that no one would be harmed. We prayed for Daddy and the firefighters and for Katherine's safety. As I held her, I could feel her relax, her rigid little body softening in my arms.

Fortunately, the fire was contained in the laundry room of the hotel. No one was injured, although our room smelled smoky, and we decided not to stay there. The hotel manager arranged for us to move for the night to another local inn, and everything was calm again.

But I never forgot the night my daughter taught me to pray.

Chapter Fifteen

You Are You

'Geh-dweh,' she said, grinning, a slice of half-eaten apple clutched in her grimy fist. 'Geh-dweh,' Get dressed. She made her pronouncement again. It was morning. We had just finished breakfast and—as Katherine reminded me—it was time to get dressed. She ran her routine like a drill sergeant. Get up. Eat breakfast. Get dressed. She timed the arrival of the bus by the sequence of the morning. When she was dressed, the bus should arrive.

'Geh-dweh. Geh-go.' Get dressed. Get going. She was nothing if not insistent. As I dressed her, she began to whine and fuss. It took us months of fear that she was in pain before we realized that we were being had. She fussed at dressing because she could hardly wait to get going in the morning, on the bus, and off to her program. She was so eager for the bus to come, eager to go to her special school. In her eagerness, the hassle of dressing could barely be endured.

Many times, Tom or I would plaintively wail back at her, 'Katherine, please stop fussing.'

One day, I tried a different tactic. I told her, 'I will do the fussing today so you don't have to.' I moaned and whined in imitation of her.

It worked. She howled with laughter as I groaned on and on. Soon she was dressed, strapped in her wheelchair, hair combed, face washed. I packed her lunch, and wrote a note for her teachers in what our family chose to call the 'School Story.' I pushed her outside to wait with her for the bus.

The day began. One more day of caring for a handicapped child. We fed her, dressed her, sent her to school, and played with her. We carried her outside to sit in the sun or to look at the stars. We took her swimming and to Burger King. We read stories and we shared our special cuddles. We managed to carve out a routine that worked, that had many moments of pleasure and joy.

And Katherine, her personality at once both feisty and tender, created much of our joy. She had an impish grin and a winning laugh. She was an ace-class manipulator of not only her parents, but also her teachers.

In the early spring, Tom and I planned to take a few days out of town together. He had a conference in Toronto, and I planned to tag along for a few days of respite. Patty Barrett and Martha Freitag, Katherine's teacher and speech therapist, respectively, had offered to care for her during our absence. We arranged for them to visit us after school so that we could walk them around our home, and fill them in on Katherine's schedule.

After the tour, we stopped in the kitchen for a snack. I handed Katherine her sippy cup with my usual instruction.

'One hand, two,' I said.

She grasped the cup with both hands and with slow, jerky movements, brought it to her lips and drank.

Martha and Patty looked at each other with wide eyes and gasped. It seems that at school, Katherine was letting the staff hold her cup while she drank. They all felt sorry for her. Not wanting her to go thirsty, they allowed Katherine to con them into helping her with something she could do for herself.

Then Katherine suddenly realized she'd been found out. Her eyes widened and a little 'mmf' sound emerged from her lips. Then, as was Katherine's way, she laughed and smiled. But nobody was going to hold her cup at school anymore, now that her teachers were aware of what she could do.

Another day, at our supper time, Katherine was reaching for her cup with one hand.

'You need two hands, Katherine,' Tom said sternly.

Katherine grasped that cup with one hand, and with all her might and concentration, pulled the cup away from her father, brought it to her lips, and drank in a fierce show of defiance.

But disability doesn't go away. It's the grief that keeps on giving. Hovering under the surface of our family life was a dull ache that said, 'This is not normal. This is not what life is supposed to be like.' And there was the constant, constant labor of taking care of a person who can do nothing for herself. Though she could bring a cup to her lips, she could not fill it herself, nor could she set it back down on the table. Tom and I developed what we called the 'right hand fly,' the movement we made in sync with Katherine as she let go of her cup, so that it would not land on the floor. Dressing, diapering, moving her — these were all our chores and instead of getting easier over time, things got more difficult as she grew and as her limits set her farther and farther apart from other children.

Sometimes even simple things brought my grief up close to the surface. I called a friend from Ann Arbor days. 'Just a minute,' she said. 'I want to move to the other phone because my children are making their breakfast beside this one.'

'My children are making their breakfast.' I wanted to talk with my friend, and suddenly I was swallowing a big gulp of grief. My daughter will never make her own breakfast. I pushed down my grief to talk to my friend. I hadn't talked to her for several months, and I had called her. I couldn't bring myself to start our conversation by telling her how her words had cut me — not by her intention, but by the reality of my experience. The intensity of my feeling was like a stab wound that sliced my soul. I carried on the conversation through a haze of the hypocrisy that happens when you hold back the full truth.

'How are you doing?'

'I'm fine.'

Not.

I shoved down the feeling in that moment, and I carried on a conversation. But now there was hollowness in it. Unfortunately, each time that my sadness emerged when I could not face it, the gap between me and the parents of the 'normal' children got wider.

Some things that were easy when Katherine was little became harder and more complicated as she grew older. What do you purchase for Christmas when your child cannot manipulate most of the toys that are on the market? In early December the Mary Cariola staff presented a seminar on toys for our children and how to find them.

Armed with a list of adaptive toys, I headed cheerfully to the toy store. But the store personnel were not particularly helpful that day and they did not recognize most of the toys on my short list. In the end, I found one of them, but not until I had plowed past the bicycles and puzzles and craft kits and Legos that filled the store, seeing them with a deep yearning that my daughter, too, could play with these things. But only a very few of the baby toys were appropriate for her. I stood in the aisle, faint with sorrow.

Church life was demanding. While I put in over fifty hours each week, it never seemed like enough. There was always more to do. One time I was accused of spending too much time with my daughter, and not enough with the church. That stung! I was able to make an adequate defense, and ultimately little harm came of that criticism. Still, I wondered what people were thinking of me, and how my family life impacted the professional work that I was able to do. And I was exhausted, carrying the burdens of my personal life as well as the burdens of my church and parishioners.

That spring, I set out for Shalom Mountain Retreat and Study Center. Shalom Mountain is a retreat center located about four hours from the Rochester area. It was founded by Jerry Jud, a United Church of Christ pastor. As a pastor myself, I was obliged to engage in continuing education; attendance at a three-day 'Shalom Retreat' would qualify.

The Shalom process begins on Thursday night with dancing, a

welcome, and time for group interaction. There is a particular emphasis on creating a community out of the varied participants who come. On the first morning, we began with yoga and meditation. Then each person was given six minutes to 'tell their story.' By lunchtime, the group coalesced into a supportive community as the depth work of the retreat began. The focus of the retreat was to release the anger, grief and fear that blocks loving relationships.

When it was my turn, I was pretty unfocused. I didn't know what 'I wanted to work on,' but that did not deter Jerry Jud from getting started. I lay down on the mat that was at the center of the room, and he encouraged me to breathe deeply. Suddenly, I discovered the rage that was flowing through my veins.

'I hate you, God,' I hollered.

Jerry urged me to continue. He told me to make fists and to pound on the mat. Then he had some of the group members hold up a padded board and let me kick hard against it.

'How could you!' I was screaming so loud my throat hurt. 'How could you let a beautiful, innocent child live with cerebral palsy! No! No! No!' Now my whole body was involved—an organism created of solid rage.

The anger poured out of every cell in my body. Each Sunday morning, I had stood in a pulpit and sweetly proclaimed the love of God. But in the deepest part of my being, I was filled with rage, sorrow, and fear. And I knew just who was responsible for my pain: the God who had created me.

Jerry was not finished. 'God is—,' he said, taunting me to finish his sentence. 'God is—'

And what I said was 'a sledgehammer.'

God is a sledgehammer.

The room where we met was loaded with props of various kinds: weird hats, work gloves, tennis rackets, drums, a sledgehammer. These things would be pulled up to enable each participant to touch and understand and express what hurt the most.

Having seen the sledgehammer before I began, it rose to my consciousness as the way I was experiencing God. Jerry handed me a sledgehammer. It was so heavy, I could barely move it. But my body was filled with an adrenaline rage and I picked up that thing and swung it. I brought it down hard on the padded board that was now lying flat in the center of the room. I brought it down again. And again.

Spent, I dropped it on the ground. Jerry picked up the mallet and quietly handed it to a member of my group of witnesses. She, in turn, passed it around the room. I had been heard.

And I had been held.

The community gathered around me witnessed my hurt and fury and they did not abandon me.

Underneath my pain and rage, a deep river of grace swelled up and swallowed me whole. In the presence of this intentional, loving community, I felt the overwhelming unconditional love that gave me life, sustained my being, and made me free. God's love. God's love for me, and God's love for Katherine.

And then I saw it: Katherine was God's child, too. Her journey is so different from mine, and so difficult. Her disabilities made my life harder, too. But we were two travelers in this life, two souls born of God's love and heading back ultimately to that place where time does not limit us and peace is fulfilled.

That night I had a dream. Katherine and I were flying. The sun was shining and we were in bliss. Even her wheelchair—the light blue one that collapsed into a car seat—was floating on air, and she called out to me, 'Mom, I don't need to walk; I can fly.'

When I finished my work on the mat, I was filled with joy. My darkest wound had seen the light of day and love flowed into it. My brokenness had been made visible, and still I was accepted. In my mind's eye, I saw Katherine, and all I could do was praise.

'You are you,' I said with fervor. 'You are you. You are *you*.'

I saw her soul, a being I loved fiercely. I understood that we were not alone in this love; it was so much larger than either of us.

'I love you. I love you, Katherine.'

I thought I heard Katherine whisper back to me, 'I love you, too.'

When the retreat was over, I went down the mountain back to reality. There would be more laundry, more surgeries, more discouraging days. But I never lost what I learned that day. Underneath all my anger and fear and grief was a love that is unconditional and boundless and sure. I went all the way into my rage at God and my bottomless grief, and discovered a sweet kindness that was fierce in its intent to find me.

The words of a hymn flew into my heart: 'And I will be with thee, thy trouble to bless / And sanctify to thee, thy deepest distress.'

***

Many years later, after we had adopted our son, we set off on a family outing. Katherine was fifteen, and Mark, a verbal, physically active five-year-old. Tom and I had bundled the kids into their car seats and we rolled out of our driveway. I breathed that maternal sigh of relief that the car was loaded and we were actually on our way.

Halfway down our street, Mark piped up.

'Mom,' he said. 'Why did God make Kaprin?'

For a minute I clutched. Katherine was right there in the car with us. And then the words came unbidden to my lips.

'Oh, Mark, honey,' I said. 'Because God loves her. Same reason God made you.'

Love. Only love.

Epilogue

I wish I could say that raising Katherine made me a better person. It made me a different person, not necessarily a better one. True, in Katherine I discovered a glimpse of God's grace that I might not have found otherwise, and discovered a world of unconditional love in the mystery of her being. Because of her, I tasted the sweet, sweet joy of service. But I also felt sorry for myself and used my difficulties as an excuse for self-indulgence, petulance and resentment.

It is my story. If Katherine told it, no doubt it would be quite different.

We were sitting at supper one night when Tom and I admitted to our mutual surprise that we were a happy family! That was the twinkle in our eyes that led us to seek Mark's adoption. And then, two incidents in quick succession motivated us further.

I had served on a state-wide committee with Harold Wilkie, a United Church of Christ pastor, born with no arms who wrote extensively on the subject of persons with disabilities. He was at the White House when George H.W. Bush signed the ADA into law. He was also nothing if not blunt. One day he turned to me and said, 'Do you have other children?'

'No,' I said. I explained that I didn't think it was possible, given the demands of Katherine's care and my professional workload.

'Oh,' he said. His eyes narrowed and he looked at me intently. 'I was always glad my parents had more children after me. I would not have wanted to live with the burden of knowing that they gave up their dreams because of me.'

I stammered something about adoption making it more difficult and took my seat at a plenary session. There I shook, literally, physically shook for 45 minutes. That was a clue that he had touched a nerve.

About the same time, my cousin told me that Harold Wiersma, the social worker who had placed Katherine in our home, was leaving that agency. The rumor was false, but before I learned that, I felt distressed. I was quite sure Harold would go to bat for us if we ever adopted again, and I wanted his support.

The combination of these two events helped me become aware of my longing to raise another child—preferably one that did not have a seriously disabling condition. So we moved forward with the roller-coaster process that is adoption, and in May, 1988, welcomed a great big bundle of baby boy into our home: Mark Edward Prins.

During the final stages of adopting Mark there were weeks of waiting and worrying and hoping that today would be the day the judge would sign the order releasing him for adoption. The agency decided to send us a picture at least, to calm our fears and help us prepare.

I stayed home the morning the Purolator Courier truck was set to arrive and was standing in the kitchen window as it slowed to a stop in front of our driveway. A quick signature and I went back into the house to get my first glimpse of our new baby. When I opened the package, I burst into tears. In their baby pictures, Mark and Katherine could be identical twins. They were adopted ten years apart in different cities and states—and they were our children.

At first, Katherine was thrilled and excited about the new baby. When she discovered that having a baby meant sharing her parents, she was not so sure. Gradually, she assumed her role as big sister, including goading him into giggles and complaining loudly when he did something she didn't like. The four of us lived happily together for the next seven years.

As Katherine entered her teen years, however, Tom and I began to feel more and more overwhelmed by her daily care. We were also stretched thin because often providing what Katherine needed meant sacrificing something Mark needed and vice versa. When we approached a group home agency for children and young people, we were told to weep loudly when we met with the director because we weren't quite needy enough. After all, we were still married and had jobs. If we lost our jobs or separated, we'd move up to the top of the line much faster. I said, 'Do we have to fall apart *before* we get help?'

When Heritage Christian Home, Inc., told us they had a placement for her, we leapt at the chance. As hard as it would be to let her go, we knew we could not continue our exhausting daily load without severe consequences to the rest of the family. Katherine moved into a local group home when she was seventeen-and-a-half years old. She was about the same age I was when I headed off for college.

Katherine knew the residents of her new home because she had met them at a church group for persons with developmental disabilities. She was happy to move in. We had a party for her in our back yard, and friends and family members came to celebrate her new life.

On the day that she moved, Tom and I were in her bedroom at the group home, unpacking her suitcases, while she was in the kitchen gurgling and chortling with the speech therapist. When we came up to her, she said, loudly, 'Guh, guh, guh.'

'Do you want a coke?' I asked.

'Guh, guh, guh.'

Okay, so it's not a coke. 'Do you want to go somewhere?'

'Nyeh,' said she. Then she started again: 'Guh. Guh. Guh.'

Finally, I turned the question around and asked, 'Do you want *us* to go? Do you want us to leave?'

'Ya-eh,' she said firmly, a little gleam in her eye.

And she had a life. A life that didn't necessarily include us at every turn.

Katherine lived at that home for fifteen years, although the other residents have changed. She was mostly happy. She attended a program each day that got her out of her house and into the community. She had a boyfriend (who lives in another nearby group home), went to church on Sunday, and welcomed her parents whenever we came.

When Mark was younger, few people would believe him when he told them his sister was 'bossy,' but they fell for it every time he asked for a second piece of candy 'for my sister.' They really got that backwards.

Mark has turned into one of the most delightful young men the world has yet to know, and I say this without an ounce of prejudice.

In June of 2009, Katherine became very ill. For the next fifteen months, she bounced back and forth between the hospital and her home. We watched helplessly as gradually she became weaker and weaker and could no longer rebound from her illnesses. She passed away on September 14, 2010, as I held her in my arms, and Tom and Mark stood by to wait, sing and pray. She is at peace.

And Tom and I are growing older . . . together.

Acknowledgements

Whenever Tom and I took Katherine to a mall, an outdoor festival or other large gathering, people we didn't know would come up to us to say hello to her. Though they were strangers to us, they were friends she made at her school programs whom she would greet with her big-hearted giggles. Throughout her life, Katherine — and her family — were assisted by many such angels. They came in the form of teachers, physicians, aides, bus drivers, and babysitters, occupational, physical and speech therapists, direct care staff, social workers and pastors. You are legion. I will never even know all your names. And you are why Katherine could have so many happy days, and why we her family, could survive. From the bottom of my heart, thank you. I do not think I would have found my hope and joy without your encouragement and daily work, and there would have been no story to tell.

As I graduated from seminary, Prof. Tom Troeger, my seminary homiletics professor invited me to lunch to give me a particular message. "You are a good writer," he said. "I want you to think about writing for publication as part of your ministry."

Well, Tom, it took almost thirty years, but here it is: a book. Thank you for the nudge all those years ago.

Thank you to Jerry Jud who cracked open my rage at God and helped me discover that God's graciousness is bigger than my despair. And thank you to the leaders and participants of Shalom Mountain Retreat and Study Center, who following in Jerry's footsteps, keep open a place of spiritual succor that nourished me again and again. A special shout out to Vyana Bergen. When I complained to her that I was not going anywhere on this project, she offered an invaluable suggestion: find a writing coach.

My deep appreciation goes to Lori Vanden Bosch, who became that coach, and to Sandy Vander Zicht, who helped me find her. Early on, Lori asked me if I *needed* to write this book. I did. Her feedback—by turns fierce, gentle and curious—helped me pull together memory and story into a coherent whole.

To my early readers: Annetta Prins, Rev. Martha Stone, Gail Elenbaas, Eleanor Elenbaas, Dr. Elaine Cleeton, Bert Wierenga, Rev. Carol Hull, Mary Speyer, Martha Tollers, Dr. Rosanne Brouwer, Peg McCracken, Ellie Bradley, Ginger Anderson, Kathy Heetderks, Colleen Kunz, Rev. Mary Frens, and Lindsay Wohlschlager: thanks for taking the time to read this story and to encourage me while I waited for the right publisher to pick up this title.

To Timothy Staveteig and Circle Books: thank you so very much for accepting my proposal with great enthusiasm. It was a huge gift to me that you were *excited* about the book; I knew I could trust you to bring it safely into the world.

Katherine: in your short life, you brought joy everywhere you went. You challenged me to think more deeply about what life really means, and you imprinted my heart with love that never leaves me.

Our son, Mark, came equipped with a large heart, a great sense of mischief and an abundance of insight. You filled our lives with more blessing than you ever can imagine.

My husband, Tom, has been part of this story from the beginning. He is the partner who hung in there with me through wrestling and rejoicing. He was generous in his support of this project, even accepting my request that he not read it until I had finished the first draft. I held my own breath as he got on a plane with the manuscript under his arm, and released it after he had landed and called me to tell me that my writing was true and the story told.

Abundant thanks for abundant blessings.

Circle Books

Circle is a symbol of infinity and unity. It's part of a growing list of imprints, including o-books.net and zero-books.net.

Circle Books aims to publish books in Christian spirituality that are fresh, accessible, and stimulating.

Our books are available in all good English language bookstores worldwide. If you can't find the book on the shelves, then ask your bookstore to order it for you, quoting the ISBN and title. Or, you can order online—all major online retail sites carry our titles.

To see our list of titles, please view www.Circle-Books.com, growing by 80 titles per year.

Authors can learn more about our proposal process by going to our website and clicking on Your Company > Submissions.

We define Christian spirituality as the relationship between the self and its sense of the transcendent or sacred, which issues in literary and artistic expression, community, social activism, and practices. A wide range of disciplines within the field of religious studies can be called upon, including history, narrative studies, philosophy, theology, sociology, and psychology. Interfaith in approach, Circle Books fosters creative dialogue with non-Christian traditions.

And tune into MySpiritRadio.com for our book review radio show, hosted by June-Elleni Laine, where you can listen to authors discussing their books.

MySpiritRadio